Stepdaughters of History

*Walter Lynwood Fleming Lectures in Southern History*

# Stepdaughters of History

## SOUTHERN WOMEN AND THE AMERICAN CIVIL WAR

## CATHERINE CLINTON

*Louisiana State University Press*
*Baton Rouge*

Published with the assistance of the V. Ray Cardozier Fund

Published by Louisiana State University Press
Copyright © 2016 by Louisiana State University Press
All rights reserved
Manufactured in the United States of America
First printing

Designer: Barbara Neely Bourgoyne
Typefaces: Chaparral Pro and Brix Slab
Printer and binder: McNaughton & Gunn, Inc.

LIBRARY OF CONGRESS CATALOGING-IN-PUBLICATION DATA

Names: Clinton, Catherine, 1952– author.
Title: Stepdaughters of history : southern women and the American Civil War /
  Catherine Clinton.
Description: Baton Rouge : LSU Press, 2016. | Series: Walter Lynwood Fleming lectures
  in southern history | "Published with the assistance of the V. Ray Cardozier Fund." |
  Includes bibliographical references and index.
Identifiers: LCCN 2016012821 | ISBN 9780807164570 (cloth : alk. paper) | ISBN
  9780807164587 (pdf) | ISBN 9780807164594 (epub) | ISBN 9780807164600 (mobi)
Subjects: LCSH: United States—History—Civil War, 1861–1865—Women. | United
  States—History—Civil War, 1861-1865—Participation, Female | Women—Southern
  States—History—19th century. | United States—History—Civil War, 1861–1865—
  Social aspects. | Confederate States of America—Social conditions.
Classification: LCC E628 .C575 2016 | DDC 973.7082—dc23
LC record available at http://lccn.loc.gov/2016012821

The paper in this book meets the guidelines for permanence and
durability of the Committee on Production Guidelines for
Book Longevity of the Council on Library Resources.

JAN 1 7 2017

*Dedicated to*

John Beecher (1986–2012)

*and*

Keith Jeffery (1952–2016)

~~~~~

*Gone too soon, and much missed by family, friends*
*and the world of scholarship which they embraced and elevated.*

# CONTENTS

# One Thousand, Four Hundred, and Fifty-Eight Days

The hard hand of war thrashed its way through the grass, uprooting traditions and leaving a trail of bruised refugees and all that remained to a scattering wind. Scared combatants foraged an unfamiliar landscape, trampling flora and fauna, disturbing any natural rhythms, as all lay bare along the banks of memory: fearful of crossing to the other side—the unknown—to perhaps defeat, and to, God forbid, retribution.

The formerly proud nation was laid low, littered with the debris of reckless ego and martial pride. The Confederate nation flourished longer in commemoration than its bleak survival of four memorable, martyred years, from secession in Charleston, from valleys to little round tops, into craters and trenches, from puddles of blood and to oceans of mud—spiraling toward the bleak, blank surrender at Appomattox: one thousand, four hundred, and fifty eight days, but who's counting?

*Who's counting* on those men who went off to protect women and children from insult, then invaders? Who's counting the months and weeks and days when those left behind mopped brows, rolled bandages, darned socks, stitched sashes, and waved handkerchiefs before resorting to using them. After the years rolled by, many began to chronicle poignant accounts of countless sacrifices and the inglorious deeds of the enemy. The writing was therapy, but the rereading could not provide cure.

And when the snakes were driven out at last, when the disbanded soldiers gave up to traipse their homeward trek, it was not an afterthought. The aftermath raised more uncomfortable truths for those who did not want to let the facts get in the way of their stories. Stories would redefine the contest for this generation, and the next, and the next after that—a rope of sand and sentiment.

Broken men returned home to a place where they had once turned over rich fertile sod, raising crops the world eagerly sought—tobacco, sugar, rice, indigo, and the mightiest of them all, King Cotton. The ships had come in, the coffers filled as planters bought, sold, shifted, and carved their claims into a sparsely settled land. As the coffers filled, the coffles filed; land-hungry settlers zigzagged the continent. Europeans imported enslaved Africans to resupply the swept acres with laborers, putting them to backbreaking work on land stripped of its native inhabitants—resourceful enough most often to escape enslavement, but not able to stave off disease and subsequent decline.

The cost to two continents was unfathomable, when people on islands and peninsulas pushed, prodded, and pummeled their way toward inheriting the earth. From sea to shining sea, prairie schooners blossomed between two oceans. Crashing up against the elements, crushing obstacles to expansionism, the settlers embarked on a stampede of greed. Supplying ports across the globe with luxury goods and necessities, these visionary, predatory settlers sprinkled mercantilism and misery along their path, while always trying to remember the best way home.

Even if it was not *their* hands getting dirty, and dirtier still, it was still their dirt. They possessed the birthright, willpower, and hubris to dictate terms—how dare anything interfere with their destiny to conquer? They could redact representation with barely a glance backward at their own pasts, because retrospect was focused tightly on the glories of ancient Rome—replete with bowing Catos and scraping Pompeys. All deference due to the patriarch, as underlings might hang onto every word as gospel, mistaking whims for wisdom, a purposeful pretense. The show was meant to mask fears of incursions from intrusive reality.

Who could not be sad to see such fertile crescents strewn with corpses? Why should these beautiful lands have become so scarred?

What had led to this disjuncture, to this brawling, sprawling blight upon the land? Was it just in man's nature? Was it always man versus nature? Because of the natural divides, not just the alleged abyss between black and white, free and slave, but additionally that most fundamental reckoning between men and women?

Women, ah women, suffered through perpetual pregnancies and multiple births, clinging for dear life to families they had to produce as the men continued their relentless charge into the wilderness, cropping and taming at every turn. Black families were savagely uprooted, with a million displaced and enchained during the decades leading up to the war.

And when the war came, white southern women were urged to pray for victory, to remain stoic in the face of blockades, abandonment, invasions, and the irregular posting of death lists. Females young and old, staring down the long barrel of life, hoping to stave off the worst of what they feared might come, as men marched off, even sallied forth. Between three and four hundred thousand of those men *never came back.* How could it ever be "getting one's own back?," as these numbers are staggering to us now and unimaginable then?[1]

In the name of Confederate independence, hundreds of thousands of boys in gray became crippled by disease and crushed by wounds, jettisoning hopes in distant fields. The result of the war was not just spoils for the victor but despoilment for the vanquished—women as well as men. The harshest threats were not bullets but lingering germs. Illness became the deadliest of foes—a rapacious hand, snatching loved ones away. Mothers and wives fought off dread. Out of five men who died while enlisted, one would die from wounds inflicted by combat, and one would die outright from a bullet or blow during armed battle. But the vast majority—three out of five—died from viral or bacterial forces, an unseen and misunderstood foe. Not blue or gray, not black or white, but disease was the *enemy,* multiplied in the name of war and only overshadowed by death.

Death used to come to the very young, and the aged, and might well strike down the sickly. But once a person had survived the perils of infancy and childhood diseases, youth was viewed as a robust and precious commodity. Hundreds, then thousands, and finally, hundreds of thousands of the young and hearty were lured into the gluttonous maw of war. This remains the Civil War's filthiest secret, that those who sacrificed were generally felled by diarrhea or gangrene—an agonizing, brutal disintegration rather than a swoop of glory.

We obsess over the Civil War dead during sesquicentennial reflections, contemplating the sheer size and scope of carnage. One hundred and fifty years later, we gasp over its human scale, the destruction demanded by this nineteenth-century inferno. Lincoln warned in his second inaugural address that it would go on "until every drop of blood drawn with the lash shall be paid by another drawn with the sword."

In recent years, we have confronted coffins shipped back from Afghanistan and Iraq, landing at Dover Airfield without fanfare. Only the names and photos scrolling down television screens have offered occasional reminders of U.S. soldiers' "untimely" deaths. Screen shot after screen shot of freshly scrubbed faces—young and old, but, oh, so many young—and when can death be deemed untimely in a combat war? Now, we recognize that the number who died in Civil War uniforms was not the generally accepted 620,000 but many more.[2] If the percentage of Civil War death was translated into equivalent numbers for today's population, Americans would face a toll of nearly 6 million dead soldiers. The scrolling of the death list would take up days, not minutes. Think how the public might howl at such a price imposed on families, on communities, on our nation.

Civil War historian James McPherson suggests, "Even if the number of war dead was 'only' 620,000, that still created a huge impact, especially in the South, and a figure of 750,000 makes that impact—and the demographic shadow it threw on the next two generations of Americans—just that much greater."[3] J. David Hacker, whose work has shifted the numbers dramatically upward, stated in the *New York Times* that his work was not done just out of curiosity: "We're seeing at least 37,000 more widows here, and 90,000 more orphans. That's a profound social impact, and it's our duty to get it right."[4]

Getting it right has been a preoccupation since the earliest days of combat. And recording death was made more immediate with the mechanical capturing of images. Intrepid photographers caught images on glass plates of silenced soldiers who could voice no objections to being shown from unflattering angles. Men, many of them really just boys, were caught in awkward, balletic poses. A generation was plucked from behind pulpits, desks, and plows and within months, if not days, pressed into the cold, hard earth. On the killing fields following combat, the sounds of the wounded, begging for water, filled the air. In delirium, many called out for their mothers, stirring even the enemy's sympathies. As pickets waited for the generals to decide who would blink first and raise the white flag so survivors might be collected from the field, soldiers died by the dozens. What took nine months to grow and nearly two decades to nurture might disappear in a flash—or, worse yet, die by inches on a roiling field of rotting, wounded flesh. In the wake of battle, families prayed for hospitalization rather than burial.

~~~~~~

All of this history and more overwhelmed me when I was contacted by the Department of History at Louisiana State University in 2010 and invited to share my work. I was in the midst of several projects and hoped I could fit one of them into my Fleming lectures: perhaps my long-time work on a study of rape and the Civil War, my idea about a short book on emancipation (abandoned), or my study of Civil War suicide (since transformed into a larger project on Union soldiers diagnosed with insanity during wartime).

But there was just the slightest hint that I might want to offer lectures on the topic of women, and how could I resist revisiting the topic of southern women and the Civil War? In the late 1980s, I toyed with the idea of writing a textbook on women and the American Civil War—prompted by several publishers who had suggested "we'd like a female *Battle Cry of Freedom*" (And *who wouldn't?*) But this undertaking was daunting, and I heard voices in my head: "I know Jim McPherson, Jim McPherson's a friend of mine, and you, Catherine Clinton, are no Jim McPherson!" I also found myself sidetracked by writing biographies when I decided in 1991 to leave the academic treadmill to write full time and spend more time with my sons, Julian Drew and Edwin Paul (then seven and two). All three of my major biographies were about women whose lives intersected with the Civil War with powerful consequences: Fanny Kemble, Harriet Tubman, and Mary Lincoln.

During my fifteen years without any permanent academic affiliation, I was haunted by Natalie Zemon Davis's brilliant insight on women being denied access to libraries in early modern Europe and the significance of their struggle to gain it. I was given such generous support, and I want to extend my personal thanks to the DuBois Institute—under the direction of Nathan Huggins, Werner Sollers, Barbara Johnson, and finally, Henry Louis Gates Jr., who gave me access to Widener Library when I needed it most. I was also offered an affiliation by the Gilder Lehrman Center for the Study of Slavery, Resistance, and Abolition, first through the kindness of David Brion Davis, who allowed me to learn to love Sterling Memorial Library, and then David Blight, who has been for several decades a comrade and cheerleader since our paths first crossed in Cambridge. These fellowships were—except for a library card—nonstipendiary, but they provided me with the tools to persist in the project of historical renovation, particularly in respect to Civil War history. In addition to wonderful visiting chairs at the University of Richmond, Wofford College, Baruch College (City University of New York), and the Citadel—and with special thanks to Claire Potter for a visiting post at Wesleyan University—I was able to continue teaching Civil War Studies while pursuing a writing career.

I should have guessed that the Civil War would put its stamp on me, as I am a recovering Civil War mascot. During the centenary in the 1960s, my parents dragged me from our Kansas City home to countless events along the Missouri border. A reluctant draftee, I won the prize for youngest participant at nearly every banquet, reenactment, or dedication attended. By the time I headed off to college, however, I'd lost my resentment of my stepfather's zeal for Civil War history.

My interest in the topic exponentially increased in the 1970s, when I began reading fascinating letters and diaries from the era. Equally compelling, Civil War photography provided alluring exposure to the haunting qualities of this war long past, while the war of my own youth, Vietnam, was being broadcast on television. However, public enthusiasm for the Civil War was in direct proportion, it would seem, to academic

indifference toward the popular interest in the conflict. As an undergraduate, I remember being advised that the diaries of the women who
fascinated me the most were *not* to be trusted: indeed I seemed to have
an affinity for alleged "fakes": Fanny Kemble's journal, Harriet Jacobs's
*Incidents in the Life of a Slave Girl*, and Mary Chesnut's reminiscences.

Long after C. Vann Woodward published *The Origins of the New South*
(1951) and *The Strange Career of Jim Crow* (1955), he went on to win his
Pulitzer Prize in 1982 for *Mary Chesnut's Civil War*. She who finally confirmed his status and reward was a captivating and convoluted storyteller
whose reminiscences were nipped and tucked on the path to publication,
as were the writings of most former Confederate women diarists. My
curiosity was piqued by how long it would take historians in this field
to discover and explore the myriad females who were buried within the
archives and scattered within popular culture but did not seem to make it
beyond the footnotes of Civil War scholarship. Some of these captivating
and capable women scribblers had faded into obscurity for decades. Many
were gifted and ambitious, yet neglected for a combination of wrong-
headed factors. Distinctive voices persisted, and I discovered that women
trapped behind the lines during the Rebellion could and did bond. But it
was mainly after the war that white women maintained strong personal
and ideological ties, when former Confederates collectively forged identities as veterans, as a band of sisters. (See Chapter 1.)

These emblematic women have been subjected to several generations
of Civil War historians keeping score. Over a century and a half later,
calculations and reconsiderations continue. The second book I published
was drawn from a lecture given as a preceptor at Princeton in the late
1970s—a project conceived out of my disappointment at women's absence
from the reading material in a course on nineteenth-century America, a
course with negligible treatment of women throughout. As I had organized a conference on women's history as a postgraduate student, funded
by the Davis Center, I wanted to imagine that it was the lack of a com-
pendium study, a narrative framework, that was preventing women from
being incorporated into the American history curriculum and textbooks.

I struggled to incorporate new and emerging work on women into
a narrative framework. Both the series editor, Eric Foner, and the pub-

lisher, the late and very-much-missed Arthur Wang, insisted that I use the title *The Other Civil War,* rather than my original, "The Other War." So I learned of the publishing world's embrace of the Civil War "ka-ching"— that old-fashioned imitation of a cash register ringing. Inevitably, while engaged in topics revolving around slavery and gender, the Civil War got stuck in my head. I literally felt it bumping round my skull, like the Elvis Costello tune, "Scarlet Tide." The war had a kind of magical realism—and haunted me. "The Civil War," those three little words, dancing just below the surface, those three little words commanding respect.

I watched my Princeton mentor James M. McPherson finish up his best-selling textbook *Ordeal by Fire: The Civil War and Reconstruction* (1982) and then pick up a Pulitzer for his *Battle Cry of Freedom* in 1989. He became a rock-star historian on the lecture circuit and has continued to turn out best sellers for more than thirty years. By the close of the 1980s, a really seismic project affected legions of us working in American history: in 1990 Ken Burns's *The Civil War* premiered on PBS.[5] (His brother Ric was a producer on the series.) I have made my critique elsewhere about its minimalist treatment of women.[6] Yet I do have to give the Burns brothers credit for setting a fire under so many scholars, and the public. The fascination of Civil War fans and buffs remains buoyant—as does the hunger for Civil War video games.[7]

In 1992, *Divided Houses* highlighted a serious disjuncture: Civil War history and women's history had too long conspired to maintain "separate but equal spheres," a situation I resisted and condemned. In a reverse "devil's lane" (a term for a disputed tract of land between two properties), the study of women during the Civil War became the neglected patch that both sides failed to claim. With newer work, I have tried to explore the ways in which sex might be a more active dynamic if it were not confined to a category of "noun." If we expand our defining terms to include gender as an analytical tool—well out of the master's hands—and sex as a verb, we can create preliminary interventions, such as *Battle Scars: Gender and Sexuality in the American Civil War.* As disturbing as this might be to a range of scholars, Civil War Studies has been undergoing previously unimaginable transformations within the twenty-first-century academy.

Most Civil War scholars remain content to tell stories in one medium, but in the twenty-first century, documentaries and live streaming expand our potential audience. The dynamics of storytelling have been altered by the Burns brothers' considerable talents and contributions—something I have contemplated when my MacBook computer asks me if I want to use the "Ken Burns effect" while preparing a slideshow.

Civil War history and women's history remain mutually exclusive domains—as I have argued vigorously in my scholarship, first with *Divided Houses* and the subsequent anthology *Battle Scars*.[8] Women have been most broadly accepted and integrated into these fields by way of those women who achieved notoriety by male standards of accomplishment—women spies, scouts, and couriers, and most especially those who had the audacity to disguise themselves as men, became soldiers, and made noteworthy contributions. (See Chapter 2.)

Thus, my reflections about southern women and the Civil War, included in the following chapters, are elliptical. I am trying to reflect not solely on the state of the field but on the opportunities for continuing the project of transformation. I may have begun my career as an integrationist, but I have evolved into an interventionist. I believe in taking every opportunity to afford women a platform, a place at the table—even if we don't like the menu. Civil War studies is being transformed by a dynamic and expanding group of younger scholars in the twenty-first century—many of whom are impatient with both my agenda and my scholarship. These fiery younger critics cannot say anything worse than what I heard about my work in the 1980s: Wasn't I just taking this or that position because I was a woman supporting a feminist agenda? Didn't I get this or that job because I was a woman? And during scholarly gang bangs: Why was I trying to turn the Old South into a brothel with my emphasis on sex? Wasn't I robbing enslaved women of their agency with my emphasis on sexual exploitation? Leaving all this aside, whatever mistakes I made—and continue to make—the overall project of historical renovation remains a bracing enterprise.

A continuing challenge is reflected in the ongoing crusade of the Civil War's scholars to engage the elusive African American audience in their quest for impact. This is a conundrum that will remain a painful puzzle for many of us excavating nineteenth-century sources. Certainly, we can begin by engaging with dismantling those conceptions of southern women which exclude or caricature black women in Civil War America. (See Chapter 3.)

For me, digging out the records for women of color such as Susie King Taylor and Frances Rollin has created a deeper and wider appreciation that we must more creatively approach our topics.[9] Working on the fascinating Loreta Janeta Velazquez with a brilliant filmmaker, Maria Agui Carter, has reinforced my interest in exploring other mediums, as well as in bringing our scholarship to larger audiences.[10] We must not hold women in the past hostage to historical standards that keep them in the sidebars and footnotes, only including those who achieve status "within a man's world." So this became an overarching project, part and parcel of my academic vocation in the waning years of the twentieth century.

A riot of rich materials unfold, as engagement exponentially multiplies. I do not want to offer the next generation of Civil War scholars a narrative framework, any straw women to toss onto the bonfire, although I look forward to reading such interventions. Fracturing and fragmentation may be better watchwords for this next generation of historians, engaged in the process of testing whether an enduring narrative should be the gold standard of the field. Not in spite of, but because of the lack of a unified whole, I am heartened by the profusion of perspectives.

The hunger for Civil War voices continues.[11] Dozens of dissertations and monographs are blazing forth, and vibrant volumes of collected letters, diaries, and journals appear with each passing year. Scholars are engaging with autobiography and bio-mythography, and these paths regularly converge, with new and improved Civil War monographs. This scholarship will enrich our past and build a better future for all our children—redheaded stepchildren as well. We cannot recapture the entire range of experience for the entire Civil War and its limitless legacy within two covers or with a dozen clicks on the Internet. But with each passing year, writers and readers can begin again—and again—revisiting the chronicles and challenges of those one thousand, four hundred, and fifty-eight days.

Stepdaughters of History

# ONE

# Band of Sisters

As the hard hand of war began to crush Confederate stalwarts' hopes of southern independence, white women who had been loyal patriots to the glorious cause of rebellion began to suspect that it was being wrecked on the shoals of slavery's destruction. As harvests and Christmas holidays rolled by, with the country still at war and dreams of victory even more elusive, these women feared deprivations would deepen when the fighting ended. Their lives would be transformed in ways they had never believed possible; those men who had led the charge for a brave new world would return home defeated to a world turned upside down.

As others have ably outlined, the war proved a trial by fire for elite southern wives, mothers, and daughters—trained to inferiority and submission. They were required to shoulder inordinate wartime burdens on the homefront, to pay lip service to an invented nation, and to pledge their loyalty with little understanding of the costs and even less preparation for the long haul. Patriotism required blindly loyal service to a country in the making. Sacrifice became the watchword.[1]

As they gave up husbands, fathers, and sons—as well as the niceties of everyday life, the security of their forebears, and the comforts to which they believed their white skin privilege entitled them—these women banded together to form a bulwark against the hopelessness that engulfed the Confederacy after Lee's retreat from Gettysburg. Mounting despair exacerbated their worsening situation through the many bloody months of loss and sacrifice.

Their band of sisters was a collective identity, even as they found themselves atomized and isolated within remote and removed communities scattered across the former Confederate States. Their story has been told and retold through progressively harsher stages of assessment from Appomattox onward, a story captivating down to this sesquicentennial generation. The roles conjured within mythmaking by and for these women excites controversy well into the twenty-first century. How and in what way women like Mary Chesnut, the Civil War's most famous diarist, intended to scribble themselves out of the morass of Confederate defeat continues to dominate war memoirs.

These dethroned plantation royalty erected a barricade, a façade incorporating remembrances of things imagined. These Confederate matrons managed to manipulate and fascinate for well over a century, providing whitewashed pageantry for audiences hungry for tantalizing tales substituting glory for truth. Rather than harping on the theme of regret, a small cadre of Confederate matrons undertook a project to mitigate fiasco. This elaborate revisionist bravado by former slaveholding women swaddled the Confederate era in nostalgia. They drowned out discordant voices with a harmonious chorus, a love song for the Lost Cause.

Chesnut may have been the most unlikely of the sisterhood to represent this Confederate choir.[2] But by the twenty-first century, she stands up to the critics and compels us to hear her distinctive voice, even if we don't heed her words. She insists readers see the world through her own idiosyncratic, dramatic, and even damaged eyes. Wrapping the post-surrender wounds in memories of days gone by, papering over the gap between what might have been and what was now the unbearable heaviness of being vanquished, Chesnut cast herself and her fellow Confederates as exiles within a landscape littered with abandoned dreams.

A culture of deceit developed in the white South—a mythology that shrouded white women in representations of cultural purity and Victorian passionlessness. These images were juxtaposed against the culture of dissemblance blacks projected to resist stereotypes of black men as Sambos and black women as Jezebels. The chivalric masquerade escalated when white women launched into a chaotic era of recovery after surrender, crafting literary sarcophagi. This charade began long before the war ended and was indeed the white sisterhood's sacred duty.

Women such as Mary Custis Lee, great-granddaughter of First Lady Martha Washington and wife of Robert E. Lee, privately expressed regrets as the forces of war unleashed. She wrote to one of her seven children from Arlington, Virginia, in April 1861: "With a sad heavy heart my dear child, I write, for the prospects before us are sad indeed, as I think both parties are wrong in this fratricidal war . . . we can only pray that in his mercy he [God] will spare us."[3] She took her duties seriously, and whatever doubts she had were not on public display. One of her Virginia friends wrote admiringly a few weeks later that "I never saw her more cheerful, and she seems to have no doubt of our success. We are looking to her husband as our leader with implicit confidence."[4]

Thus the Roman matron model of Confederate womanhood arrived fully formed in war's earliest months, exalted by leading women intellectuals such as Louisa McCord and Augusta Jane Evans.[5] They were not just the bandage-wielding bonnet brigades of Mary Elizabeth Massey's centenary study of women and the Civil War; patriotic response and interlocking legacies framed their historical campaigns. Massey's pioneering volume contains topics ripe for intervention, revision, and definitely further expansion.[6]

Stephanie McCurry has made a powerful case for twenty-first-century scholars to look to the example of Antigone. In Sophocles' rendition of Thebes, Antigone was willing to perform the death rites for her traitorous brother who led a foreign army against his king, just as she did for her other slain brother, an honored patriot. She concludes, "Antigone is a powerful representation of women's primal obligation to the realm of kinship, not citizenship; household, not polity; family, not state."[7] She posits these obligations, and the robust expectations that went along with such roles, as central for Confederate women.

Females were designated the moral compasses within plantation society. White women were to be vessels of purity and piety, while black women were subjected to prurience. All yielded to patriarchal dictates to uphold slaveholders' order. War disrupted these lines of authority, however. Wartime duty compelled women to take on roles they previously might have refused. Eliza Fain, a planter's wife in East Tennessee, reluctantly led her family in prayer, a role she at first assigned to an enslaved male during her husband's absence. But she was finally ready to act: "I have long felt the importance of keeping this duty up in the absence of my dear husband but the cross has always seemed to be too great. I trust I shall from this time forward be enabled to do my duty."[8]

In her prizewinning volume *Mothers of Invention* (1996), Drew Gilpin Faust has suggested that the Civil War meant plantation women for the first time assumed supervisory duties and other responsibilities, which had dramatic effects on wartime society. This echoes the earlier scholarship of Anne Firor Scott, among others, that claimed that women were absent from the managerial landscape until war brought about the necessary evil of female mastery, with women taking men's places at the helm of plantation administration.[9]

Faust chronicles how wartime challenges forced Confederates to abandon delicacy as the need for pragmatism outweighed propriety.[10] Matrons undertook heroic war work while keeping their homesteads running smoothly. Sacrifices were expected, and military needs trumped family interests. As Sallie Moore recalled, "We had even cut up our carpets into lengths and sent them to camps for the soldiers to sleep on."[11] As the war went on, those military needs escalated. Louisa Henry wrote in 1864 from rural Mississippi: "Our stock of cloth laid up for the negroes is almost exhausted, having given suits of clothes to the soldiers. We also have given hundreds of pairs of socks, the amount of 500 I think to the Army. Some three or four weeks since we sent twelve blankets, eight dozen pairs of socks, three carpet blankets, to Genl. Prices Army."[12] As military defeats mounted, sacrifices became increasingly onerous.

Key to her argument, Faust documents Confederate women's waning support for the war effort. Those left behind to manage resented the scarce resources, crumbling communities, and depleted energies. With such a large percentage of eligible southern men serving in the military (estimates are as high as three out of four southern white males), females in the South were indeed thrown back on their own resources.

Prior to the war, Faust suggests, elite females led protected lives in the bubble of the private sphere. Many women felt betrayed when male leadership did not fulfil its part of the bargain. The beleaguered Lizzie Neblett of Texas, anchored on her estate with eleven slaves, complained, "I am sick and tired of trying to do a man's business when I am nothing more than a contemptible poor piece of multiplying human flesh tied to the house by a crying young one, looked upon as belonging to a race of inferior beings."[13] Neblett would also despair over disobedient enslaved workers, farming out to a male neighbor the job of administering slave whippings.

Hundreds of Confederate wives testified to the trauma associated with invading Yankees and military occupation.[14] Dolly Lunt of Covington, Georgia, bemoaned repeated home invasions: "like famished wolves they come, breaking locks and whatever is in their way."[15] Attacks on property were often accompanied by personal violence. Cordelia Scales, on her plantation near Holly Springs, Mississippi, described a visit from Kansas Jayhawkers: "They tore the ear rings out of ladies ears, pulled their rings and breast pins off, took them by the hair; threw them down and knocked them about. One of them sent me word that they shot ladies as well as men & if I did not stop talking to them so & displaying my confederate flag, he'd blow my brains out."[16] These abandoned women struggled to preserve as much as they could out of the old order—to survive in this new world marred by deprivation and challenged by black struggles for freedom.[17]

Faust suggests that the majority of women who wrote about these transformations (during wartime, as opposed to postwar reminiscences) did not view added responsibilities as an opportunity for empowerment, as some modern day scholars might interpret. The women enduring these ordeals did not perceive their sacrifices as any badge of honor but rather saw them as wounds, which might even become scars. Lucy Buck warned in her Front Royal diary in 1862, "We shall never any of us be the same as we have been."[18] Faust emphasizes the relative innocence of most planter women and creates an image of war ripping away the veil; Louisianan Sidney Harding "used to think I would like to be poor but having never seen any poor people before I did not know what it was. Have no such wish now."[19]

Faust claims that in white men's absence, plantation mistresses were disillusioned by both the drudgery and the psychological stress of management.[20] She has forcefully concluded that women's disillusionment hardened into resentment, perhaps even resistance, and that there was definitely a loss of will for Confederate women over the course of the war. Some scholars quibble over concomitant conclusions about this claim, expressing a range of skepticism. Some dissenting views suggest her claims are overstated due to her narrow sample; some charge her with a failure to address adequately differentials of age, marital status, education, region, and other variables. Nevertheless, Faust's analysis has become the prevailing historiographical view of southern white women's wartime experience.[21]

What has proven much more controversial to Civil War studies is Faust's suggestion that this failure of will on slaveholding women's part contributed significantly to Confederate defeat.[22] Several other topics have emerged in recent scholarship—questions of Confederate desertion, Unionism within the wartime South, and the deep and wide ripple of southern dissenters—contributing to a reassessment of the role of "will" in wartime politics.[23] This debate over the measure of "significance" has breathed new life into historiographical disputes.

How significant was will, when was it significant, and other questions converge into lively discussions, but clearly Faust made a strong argument for women's participation and support as a key element in the war's outcome. In the wake of this historical debate, scholars have refocused their energies on the criticality of the home front to Civil War progress. Indeed, from the scholarly interventions of Elizabeth Fox-Genovese's study of plantation households in 1988 to Stephanie McCurry's look at yeoman's households in 1995, the household has emerged as a new locus of energy for Civil War scholarship. This new topic was highlighted at a panel during the Southern Association of Women Historians meeting in June 2015 in Charleston, South Carolina.[24] LeeAnn Whites has suggested that the years 1861 to 1865 constituted "a household war" in America. Interlocking perspectives on gender and race are illuminated by closer examination of shifting relations and conflicts within southern households during this critical era.

McCurry's most recent study of the war focuses on the not-so-subtle irony of the Confederacy as "a slaveholder's republic"—a secessionist country where a population of 11 million included 3 million slaves; at least half of these totals were women. Thus, the white male minority who brokered a revolution with a declaration of secession in 1861, McCurry suggests, was forced to allow the "unenfranchised" to voice their dissent.[25] Upon acknowledging these voices, not surprisingly, many "Confederate reckonings" emerge. Thus, requesting government assistance became a clarion cry for the soldiers' wives, invoking what McCurry calls a "politics of subsistence."[26] Women did not see themselves as seeking charity, she suggests, but rather framed their claims against the state as entitlements, if not rights.[27]

Further, much like Faust's elite women, McCurry's protagonists are overwhelmingly involuntarily drafted into service: "It was not so much that white women emerged incisively out of the recesses of the household into public life during the war as that the state came barging in their front door, catapulting them into a relationship they had never sought but could hardly refuse."[28] Impressment, taxes, and other policies alienated large swaths of the Confederacy, and poor women saw the government-imposed tithe on harvests as a Draconian measure. Such state imposition might tilt Confederate families from subsistence into starvation. In response, white women besieged governors with petitions.

After several seasons of war, southern storekeepers were on guard against frustrated women willing to liberate goods to feed their families. Even the Confederate president was forced into the streets to read the riot act in April 1863. To restore order, Jefferson Davis approved the distribution of flour from government storehouses to appease the women of the Richmond Bread Riot.[29] The government, fearing more uprisings and reprisals, forbade press coverage; as one Virginia woman confided, "not one word has been said in the newspapers about it."[30]

That rioting women might bring the Confederate capital to its knees was certainly news.[31] That the government feared female rebellion was deemed worth suppressing at the time, but these and other matters have remained in the sidebars of Civil War history, despite their increasingly center-stage role in southern women's history. Within traditional Civil War scholarship, female contributions remain marginalized, although there seems to be a growing effort to blend social history and military history in curriculum, textbooks, and popular culture. Confederate women still present a puzzle to most scholars of the era, but they remain a powerful subset within the catchall of "southern women." They ironically have a larger fan base in Civil War studies than their more notable northern sisters. Northern white women generally are given more coverage within both American women's history and the American survey textbook.

A study of Civil War textbooks notes that books on southern women seem to dominate in the field, outnumbering those on northern women by a wide margin.[32] (Sadly, this is not attributable to any abundance of work on nineteenth-century African American southern women, those most dramatically affected by the Civil War's outcome; this literature may be growing but remains underdeveloped.)[33]

A study of Civil War textbook adoption concentrated on required texts for nearly two hundred sample syllabi from 2000 to 2006.[34] The researchers found that a single author, James M. McPherson, has dominated the undergraduate Civil War course text market in colleges and universities, North and South. Either *Ordeal by Fire* or *Battle Cry of Freedom* was assigned as a required reading on nearly 60 percent of the syllabi. The authors also noted that at the sixty institutions where a Reconstruction text was assigned, 60 percent of the instructors chose Eric Foner's *A Short History of Reconstruction*. The authors also suggested that nearly 20 *percent* of the instructors included "one work that covered women or American slavery."[35] This token social history slot, the authors suggested, often reflected complex dynamics on the matter of sex and the Civil War textbook: "By and large, almost every textbook that explored women's role during the Civil War favored Southern women over their Northern counterpart. The major agent in over half of these works was the Southern belle."[36]

A puzzling pronouncement: "the major agent . . . was the Southern belle." Yet this prominence assigned to a Confederate female role model follows on from a century of complex interlocking historical and literary efforts—efforts that began with Rebel women who survived the war and, with deadly purpose, took up their pens. It is a familiar but fairly accurate saw that the South lost the war but won the peace. The triumphant aspects of Lost Cause ideology created a powerful historical legacy, and women's roles within this campaign have attracted attention for the past few decades.

At the turn of the twentieth century, a group of like-minded southern women were dedicated to the principle that they might write themselves out of the doldrums of Confederate defeat. Several generations of literary critics have demonstrated the nostalgic legacy of these plantation memoirs. Studies of southern fiction and memoir highlight women's distinctive roles, from Edmund Wilson's *Patriotic Gore: Studies of the Literature of the American Civil War* (1962) to Anne Goodwyn Jones's *Tomorrow Is Another Day: The Woman Writer in the South, 1859–1936* (1981), to Sarah Gardner's *Blood and Irony: Southern White Women's Narratives of the Civil War, 1861–1937* (2003) and Caroline Janney's *Remembering the Civil War: Reunion and the Limits of Reconciliation* (2013).[37] Many of the women discussed in these studies were leading intellectuals in their communities before the outbreak of war expanded their platforms and opened up dramatic possibilities, especially with the Confederate defense of the homeland under blockade and siege.

One of the leading figures of this group who comprised the collective voice of Confederate women was Augusta Jane Evans Wilson. Wilson had been born into an aristocratic family in Columbus, Georgia, the first of eight children born to Matthew and Sarah Evans. Her father's speculation forced the family into bankruptcy, and in 1837, the Evans family relocated—first to Alabama in the early 1840s, then to San Antonio, Texas, in 1846. But after the war with Mexico, Augusta's father settled his growing family in Mobile, Alabama. Young Augusta was tutored by her mother, and her love of literature led her to try her hand at writing. Her first novel, *Inez: A Tale of the Alamo* (1855), was a commercial disappointment. This was a setback, as she had hoped her career might help to support her family.

But her second effort, *Beulah* (1859), was a critical and commercial success. With the royalties from the sale of more than twenty thousand copies in the book's first nine months, she was able to purchase a house in Mobile, Georgia Cottage. She also planned to sail for the Continent and became engaged to New York editor James Spaulding. But before any of these dreams—a wedding, a European tour—came true, the Civil War intervened. Her ardent Confederate patriotism caused her to break off her engagement and to devote herself to the Confederate cause.

She threw her talents and energies into a volume reflecting the ideals of Confederate womanhood. *Macaria*, published in 1864, became an overnight success. The novel's title is taken from a mythological character, the daughter of Heracles, who sacrifices herself to the gods to prevent the invasion of Athens. Evans used her own wartime experience (copying some of her letters directly into the text) to embroider her tale of two motherless daughters, Irene Huntingdon (an heiress) and Electra Grey (a poor orphan). One girl studies astronomy, while the other takes up painting, and both are—as cliché would have it—in love with the same man, Electra's cousin, Russell Aubrey.

This tale of love and honor unfolds with dilemmas galore as Irene refuses to follow her father's wish that she consent to an arranged marriage. Electra defies the dictates of propriety as well, and both women deny themselves suitors to perform patriotic duties. Irene devotes herself to nursing Confederate soldiers, an echo of Evans's own choice. The melodramatic tale of these two young women offered the ideal of sacrifice but also created an honorific aura around women's self-sufficiency, as necessity allowed the emergence of two autonomous heroines.

During the war, Evans scribbled that "the southern matron accustom(s) herself to having every office in the household performed by others; while she sits passive and inert, over a basket of stockings, or the last new novel. . . . Southern women have more leisure for the cultivation of their intellects, and the perfection of womanly accomplishments."[38] Such a distortion baffles. Evans's sketch could be parodic, or it could be the face of defiance, braving the shoals of defeat on the horizon. I might suspect the latter rather than the former, as when Evans had to confront her family's decline and impending poverty, there was little satire.

Personally drawn into the cycle of sacrifice, the surrender in 1865 left Evans depressed, and the Civil War rendered her impoverished. Her immediate family had all survived the war, but her beloved brother Howard ("Bud") was permanently disabled. She wrote in October 1865, "I shudder at the bitter, bitter feelings I find smoldering in my heart. . . . I feel that I have no country, no house, no hope in coming years, and I brood over our hallowed precious past, with its chrism of Martyr blood."[39] She could not embrace defeat but felt nearly embalmed by it.

However, when she took her brother Bud to New York to find a specialist to treat the paralysis in one of his arms, Evans discovered that one of her Manhattan publishers had held her royalties from sales of *Macaria* in the North. Stunned by the windfall, she decided to renew her energies, to capitalize on literary success.

In 1867, she published the most successful of all her novels, *St. Elmo*. In it, Evans depicted a moral struggle between good and evil. St. Elmo Murray, the novel's protagonist, is converted to Christianity through his love for the virtuous heroine, Edna Earle. When Edna marries Murray, she happily sacrifices her literary career—a choice that illuminates Evans's cherished endorsement of women as rulers of hearth and home, a completely conventional view. Despite her own domestic independence as a thirty-year-old author with no husband (at the time), Evans preached that women were happier if they devoted themselves to domesticity. For Evans, it was an article of faith that women were happiest if they devoted themselves to their families and homes—a common ideal at midcentury and one of the major themes of nineteenth-century domestic fiction.

In 1868, at the age of thirty-three, Augusta accepted the proposal of retired Confederate colonel Lorenzo Madison Wilson. The sixty-year-old widower was a successful businessman, and he moved his bride into his Mobile mansion, Ashland, where she served as stepmother to his daughter Fannie. As mistress of a prosperous domain, the new Mrs. Wilson became a patron of several charities and an ardent gardener. However, she did not abandon her career (as her heroine Edna Earle had done). Augusta Evans Wilson would publish three additional novels: *Vashti; or, Until Death Us Do Part* (1869), *Infelice* (1875), and *At the Mercy of Tiberius* (1887). The novels had a following, although they did not measure up to the success of her earlier fiction.

Her conservatism and extreme religiosity informed her domestic fiction. Wilson was a vocal opponent of women's suffrage and a proponent of "romantic idealism," which literary critics have pointed out led her to create artificial characters and didactic plots. Nevertheless, she continued to be a prolific and respected voice of the South, a woman who most often confined her heroines to traditional roles of sacrifice and simplistic moral conventions.

Evans remained a Confederate stalwart. When a friend suggested that the war might have proven that secession was wrong, Evans replied passionately in October 1866: "The right of Secession is more holy than five years ago,—for now it has been sanctified—baptized anew, with the blood of our Legion of Liberty's Martyrs."[40] Her devotion to this cause was religious, unwavering, suffused with blood politics. She was part of the cadre of neo-Confederates who maintained an utmost faith in the Lost Cause.

Gaines Foster and Charles Reagan Wilson have demonstrated that such evangelical fervor grew in the months that followed the war's bitter close. Memories and talent allowed Wilson a route back through to the future; she became one of the most successful southern writers in the postwar era. Surely, she was the most popular southern woman writing, and her work earned her over $100,000 in her lifetime.[41]

Most women of her generation did not even attempt to follow in Evans's footsteps, although many consumed and championed celebrations of true daughters of the South with political literary agendas. White women served a special role in collective literary projects, including the establishment of the Confederate Memorial Literary Society, chartered in 1890 (with an all-female board), and the United Daughters of the Confederacy (UDC) essay contests, designed to promote the "true history" of the Civil War. While male veteran societies were declining at the turn of the century, the United Daughters of the Confederacy grew its membership from 17,000 in 1900 to nearly 70,000 by 1920. Part of its mission was to "collect and preserve materials for the truthful history of the war." This included correcting what it considered the misuse of the term "Civil War" by substituting the preferred usage of "War Between the States" or, more belligerently, "War for Southern Independence" or "War of Northern Aggression."

Revising history became a therapeutic way to stem the tide of historical forces, which neo-Confederates felt were working against them.[42]

With history always repeating itself, many Confederates wanted to break the cycle of surrender and defeat. The rise of the Lost Cause movement has been chronicled extensively by notable scholars, including Rollin Osterweis, Gaines Foster, Charles Reagan Wilson, John Coski, Cynthia Mills, Pamela H. Simpson, Karen Cox, Gary Gallagher, W. Scott Poole, and W. Fitzhugh Brundage.[43]

Confederate women's experiences have been interrogated by a fine cadre of southern historians, including the aforementioned Faust and McCurry, as well as Thavolia Glymph, LeeAnn Whites, Nell Irwin Painter, Laura Edwards, Julia Stern, Mary De Credico, Elisabeth Muhlenfield, Lisa Frank, Giselle Roberts, and Victoria Ott, to name a few leading specialists.[44] The comments and appraisals that follow are not intended to quarrel, correct, or refine per se; they are just observations drawn from my decades of engagement with the subject.[45] As I expand on familiar themes here, I want to remind myself and others of so much that is left to be done, despite what has been accomplished.

Indeed, much of what I had to say about this genre of Confederate female literary memoir found its way into print twenty years ago in a slim volume, *Tara Revisited: Women, War, and the Plantation Legend* (1995). I was fascinated by African American women writers from this period, and I have suggested that we need more studies of black women who left us testimony about their wartime experience, including Susie King Taylor and Frances Rollin, about whom I have written.[46]

We know from even preliminary investigations that battlefront and home front at times collided. We know that Civil War studies and women's history have had a long and checkered past and are finally beginning to respond to one another's clarion calls. Several opportunities will be missed without collaboration in the Civil War field and a new generation of blended priorities. Indeed, both subfields have been successful at capturing the public's imagination and will hopefully continue to beguile book buyers.

When we look back at the era of the Civil War, remarkable stories invite further exploration. During wartime, women might get in the way of men waging war. Loreta Janeta Velazquez reflected in her autobiography: "The ground is so thickly strewn with dead . . . what a fearful thing this human slaughtering is."[47] Even as soldiers marched off to protect their hearth and home from harm, the battle might be brought right into the boudoir: Judith Henry, a bedridden widow, was killed by an artillery shell near Manassas (at the Battle of Bull Run) in 1861.[48] She is just one of the scores of emblematic women whose tragic encounters with war require closer attention. Many back roads should be traversed again—the valley of the Shenandoah, the swath of land between Atlanta and Savannah, and so many contested terrains turned into bloody war zones.

The collateral damage of civilian death was a horror to nineteenth-century eyewitnesses. Perhaps no place provided such a vivid example of dire circumstances as the Confederate holdout of Vicksburg, which fell after two years of war. A score of civilians were slain by artillery during this siege, and among the survivors forced into the caves above the hills of Vicksburg in the summer of 1863 was Mary Anne Loughborough. Even before the war ended, she published her memoir of her harrowing experience, *My Cave Life in Vicksburg.*[49]

By May 1863, Gen. Ulysses S. Grant had surrounded the city with troops, while naval forces bombarded from the river. Loughborough was a fairly new arrival to Mississippi, having fled Missouri at age twenty-seven with her husband, a major in the Confederate army, and her two-year-old daughter. When Union troops neared, the family took precautions and headed for the hills, trying to stay safe inside the caves on the bluffs overlooking the town. Loughborough's blow-by-blow coverage of the siege of Vicksburg is as riveting as any military accounts: "the rushing and fearful sound of the shell as it came toward us. As it neared, the noise became more deafening; the air was full of the rushing sound; pains darted through my temples; my ears were full of the confusing noise; and, as it exploded, the report flashed through my head like an electric shock, leaving me in a quiet state of terror."[50]

Her dramatic renditions of Yankee incursions included a heart-stopping incident:

> A Parrott shell came whirling in at the entrance, and fell in the centre of the cave before us all, lying there smoking. Our eyes were fastened upon it, while we expected every moment the terrific explosion would ensue. I

pressed my child closer to my heart, and drew nearer to the wall. Our fate seemed almost certain. The poor man who had sought refuge within was most exposed of all. With a sudden impulse, I seized a large double blanket that lay near, and gave it to him for the purpose of shielding him from the fragments; and thus we remained for a moment, with our eyes fixed in terror on the missile of death, when George, the servant boy, rushed forward, seized the shell, and threw it into the street, running swiftly in the opposite direction.[51]

After nearly fifty days of shelling, sacrifice, and impending starvation, the Confederate generals voted to surrender, and white flags began to appear on July 3, 1863. Lenient terms of peace were cemented with a truce on the anniversary of Independence Day.

Loughborough was able to publish her memoir with a New York publisher in the next year. There was a craving to know the news, to get an eyewitness account—a dramatic rendition of a ringside seat—while the Confederacy continued to crumble. This was how Augusta Jane Evans could scribble Confederate propaganda and find a northern audience for her domestic fiction. The southern white sisterhood wanted to broadcast the horrors they endured; the litany, the recitation, the recapitulation was intended to dull the pain.

White women trapped in caves or stranded on farms and plantations knew the home front was their crucible. Women's narratives of war included, in large part, not just reflections of what was lost but fears of what was still to come, as well as hopes and dreams for what might be recovered. Some, like Margaret Johnson Erwin in rural Mississippi, suffered nightmares: "In my sleep last night I saw this place levelled, and ran from tree to tree trying to find at least one child. But there was no one—child or adult. Each day I make a staunch resolution that I will not listen to one more word concerning this foolish war." But war news was all people talked about, and she was unnerved by hearing about the "disaster of Antietam."[52]

Erwin's unhappy marriage compounded her concerns. When her husband gambled and came home drunk, she made him sleep in their dead son's room, hoping that "the sight of it on an awakening may bring the man to his sense, his sense of responsibility."[53] At the age of forty-three, she wrote, "The mirror says . . . [I] have not aged much, outwardly. Inwardly I feel but a husk, useless, deprived of my friends, happy of my children, but less than satisfied with my marital state."[54] As the war wore on, she predicted, "Our real problems will come when this holocaust is over."[55] Erwin never had to face this prospect, as she died a month later.

The melancholy women I have encountered during my decades in southern women's history have often been heartrending.[56] Particularly moving accounts of women's sufferings appear in the WPA narratives and the published volumes of the Freedman's Bureau project. Mary Vaughn, who had lost her father, her husband, and one child already, wrote in February 1863 from her Virginia plantation (ironically named Sunnyside): "I have but one wish and that is to die. You speak of my baby. Why, sister, will not God smite me there too? Will he not darken my young life to the utter most? I will crush back the love, welling up in the depths of my heart for the little one, so when God lays his chilling hand upon her limbs, it will not craze me. I have not read my bible since Charlie died. My tears and feelings seem frozen. I know, I feel but one thing, I am alone, utterly desolate."[57] The suicidal young widow renamed her baby girl "Charlie," giving this child her late husband's name as she struggled on with her grief. The poignant prose of countless Confederate women continues to fascinate—although Civil War scholarship requires more incorporation of the voices of enslaved women, and will be amended by a new generation of scholars trampling out the vintage.[58]

Yet perhaps even more intriguing are the personal chronicles of a self-conscious group sharing with the world their innermost thoughts— edited, of course, for effect. This literature is studded with volumes saved from the dustbin. Much first-person literature surpasses efforts by historians struggling to capture the era because of the immediacy and impact of a voice. In many ways, it is the tone of intimacy which defeats scholars' attempts. Historians are strait jacketed, while novelists and memoirists shed considerations like balance and evidence.

Southern writer Augusta Jane Evans resisted the entreaties of Alexander Stephens, former vice president under Jefferson Davis, to take on what he considered a sacred project, writing a history of the Confederacy. She wrote in November 1865, "Permit me to say to you candidly, that although I have been repeatedly solicited to undertake it, I doubt my intellectual credentials for this grand mission."[59] She and sister scribblers declined offers to write "objectively." Their accounts were meant to be personal, tales to wrench emotions from readers. Reminiscences and memoirs poured forth, eagerly consumed in the North as well as abroad, with the craze for such literary productions peaking at the turn of the century.[60] (Although the treatment of Civil War experience in fiction would peak in the third decade of the next century, with the success of Margaret Mitchell's *Gone With the Wind*.)

The autobiographical and fictional output of this band of women writers reflected the most heroic aspects of memorialization, mirroring Lost Cause ideology. Evans's 1864 novel *Macaria* is an exemplar of this, catching the zeitgeist before it was fully formed. Confederate women's campaigns of resuscitation were underway halfway through the war, even before the stacking of arms began. Most impressive were the female characters immortalized in John Thompson's verse and William D. Washington's painting *The Burial of Latané*. This image has come to symbolize Confederate sacrifice, but it also illustrates visually the idea of a "band of sisters." J. E. B. Stuart's famous June 1862 evasion of McClellan's army in the Peninsula campaign has become part of military folklore. Confederates valorized the death of a young Virginia cavalry officer, Capt. William Latané, commemorated in a poem published in the *Southern Literary Messenger:*

> No man of God might read the burial rite
> Above the "rebel"—thus declared the foe
> That blanched before him in the deadly fight,
> But woman's voice, in accents soft and low,
> Trembling with pity, touched with pathos, read
> Over his hallowed dust the ritual of the dead—

After Latané died, a woman on a nearby plantation promised the fallen captain's brother that he would receive a proper burial. When a slave was dispatched to fetch a local clergyman, Union pickets reportedly prevented any white man from crossing the lines. Deprived of a pastor, Mrs. Willoughby Newton read the funeral service for Latané so that the promise of her sister-in-law, Mrs. William Brockenbrough, was fulfilled.

So this band of sisters performed nobly—whether it was because of or in spite of the absence of white men, a key factor forging these new bonds of sisterhood.

After this episode was venerated in verse, William Washington created a thirty-six-by-forty-six-inch oil canvas, reimagining the scene. The Confederate heroines—with their eyes shifted upward to implore the Lord to rescue them from earthy indignities—draw the viewer's eye to the center. Angelic children surround a flower-strewn grave. Whites are clearly the featured players, while the main figure—the white male—is conspicuous in his absence: there, but not there, confined to the coffin. White females and African Americans gather to bury this fallen hero— defeated by Yankees, defeated by death. As in southern paintings from portraits of George Washington's family forward, African Americans were employed as symbols that emphasized the status and significance of the foregrounded whites.[61]

In Richmond, at the Virginia state capitol, William Washington's canvas was put on display in 1864. Money was collected in a bucket placed underneath the painting to solicit charity for needy Confederate families. Steel engravings of this scene became popular after the war. By 1871, *Southern Magazine* offered a free copy with every subscription. Drew Gilpin Faust argues that the prints became the "standard decorative item in late-nineteenth-century white southern homes."[62]

*The Burial of Latané* was a graphic reminder of war's toll, tugging at heartstrings while extolling female virtue. Only women and enslaved men bid farewell to this fallen hero. Strikingly, the black male figure in the painting—slouching on his shovel—does not seem too perturbed by the exit. He appears nonchalant, indifferent, perhaps even relaxed and in repose. The action figure for the secessionist cause is decidedly unavailable. His loyal subjects bury him, with a tableaux intended to inspire sacred memory. But the white man remains in the box—and gone from the scene, both literally and figuratively.

Whether they hated the white flag of surrender or embraced war's end, women strode out into the field for a renewed war of propaganda. Even southern white women who blamed men for defeat and despised the wages of war were not content to let the Cause, nor the memory of those who died for such, fade. They pioneered enormously influential and significant memorial movements, as scholars Karen Cox, Cynthia Mills, Pamela Hemenway Simpson, and Caroline Janney, among others, have demonstrated.[63]

Confederate women's memorial movements were passionate, empowering channels for resisting erasure and defeat. Indeed, memorial campaigns by the United Daughters of the Confederacy (UDC) produced dramatic results, with Confederate monuments erected in twenty-seven states—Virginia ranking at the top with 223, and Georgia in second place with 145. From the Jefferson Davis Memorial Highway in San Diego to a lone Confederate tablet in Montana, twelve hundred markers and statues demonstrate the concerted efforts of several generations of descendants of Civil War survivors.[64]

The tributes Confederate women midwifed cast a wide spell, as the chronicles, characters, dramas, and particularly melodramas expanded exponentially in the years following Union victory. Literally thousands of pages were produced by these proud, loyal ambassadors from the land-of-what-might-have-been. These women bedazzled with their sleights of hand, as colonial poet Anne Bradstreet complained in one of her early verses: "Who said in my hand a needle better fits?"[65]

Women may not have been able to put down their needles, but they certainly took up their pens. Investing time and energy to scratch out their stories, they did not know if their efforts might end up disappearing or being erased. Yet scads of women's writings survived. The scores of titles in print thus far collectively demonstrate the war's most human aspects, including an intense strain of sisterhood, a sisterhood that may be politically incorrect, but sisterhood nonetheless.

In Baton Rouge, a young girl named Sarah Morgan began her journal in January 1862.[66] Her brother had been killed in a duel in April 1861, just as the Confederacy launched its bid for independence. This led three of Morgan's brothers to enlist in the Rebel forces. She was mourning one brother's death and bemoaning the others' enlistments when her father, a prominent attorney and judge, died unexpectedly. Left behind on several fronts, the nineteen-year-old Morgan turned to her diary as a deeply emotional outlet.

Luckily for Civil War scholars and Louisiana historians, Morgan wrote a vivid recreation of her world, with lively sketches of the war zone and refugee life. Her literary skills included recreating dramatic interludes— moonless skies and darkened wood—as well as verbatim scenes, replete with dialogue. Her renderings of her two-story frame home in Baton Rouge make it appear comfortable and intimate, whereas the war is depicted as a vast, distant abstraction. In 1861, the Battle of Bull Run confirmed Confederates' sense of superiority, but by the arrival of Union gunboats in Louisiana waters in May 1862, families took fright—and took flight. With the approach of the Yankees, Morgan's family hid out at the State Asylum for Deaf and Blind before heading toward Linwood, twenty miles north of Baton Rouge and just five miles from Port Hudson.

In August 1862, Sarah was putting on her hoops and collecting her things when shells began to "burst over the roof." Two more exploded nearby, and she heard her mother call, "Sarah! You will be killed! Leave your clothes and run!" She tried to speed up packing but was hard pressed to fit in all necessaries in the rush. Her days and nights were interrupted by warnings again and again, and she became practiced at evasion on horseback. These gypsy conditions overwhelmed, as she wrote in September: "Will I ever again have a desk or a table to write on? At present, my seat is a mattress, and my knee my desk; and that is about the only one I have had since the 2nd of August."[67]

She would become a vivid writer, a columnist, and, following the death of her husband, a nomad again. Watching events unfold, a witness to her generation's losses, she spilled out her emotions on paper. In the midst of family separations, economic upheavals, and constant reminders of life's fragility, she committed thoughts to paper, leaving powerful testimony for subsequent generations. She toted her private manuscript from home to home, filling up nearly six volumes. It was difficult to safeguard literary treasures while on the run, and it was the loyal sisterhood that most often brought these documents to light later. At one point, Mary Chesnut, unable to finish her project, sent the manuscript to a friend's house for safeguarding, where it remained entombed for over a quarter century.

Once the Civil War was over, Sarah Morgan abandoned recordkeeping and claimed not to have looked at her journals again until the 1890s, when she had a dispute with a Yankee over some minor military matter and consulted her eyewitness testimony to prove her point. Other than this irregular consultation, the manuscript remained untouched, not for public consumption. She was unwilling to relive difficult days, and reluctant to share. Instead of consigning her manuscript to the flames, she gave it to her adult son, instructing *him* to burn it. Once his mother was gone, he published it posthumously, including his own introduction and some correspondence. The book appeared in 1913 and has been a staple on Civil War reading lists for over a century. The vibrancy of Morgan's powerful testimony remains for us today.[68]

Another compelling Civil War diarist, Kate Stone, was twenty years old in 1861, when secessionist conflict extended into Madison Parish in northeastern Louisiana. More than a thousand acres and 150 slaves supported thirty-six-year-old widow Amanda Stone at her family estate, Brokenburn. Amanda had planned a European excursion for a handful of her children (she had seven surviving out of ten), but the Stones' grand tour was postponed indefinitely when, as in Sarah Morgan's case, three brothers marched off to war.[69] Amanda's daughter Kate suggested, "We who stay behind may find it harder than they who go."[70]

The fight to control the Mississippi throughout 1862 and into 1863 drove prices up and neighbors out. Even when Union troops overran nearby Milliken's Bend, Kate Stone's family dug in. During this entrenchment, they were subjected to constant harassment, as Stone recalled after a raid: "We had all just come in from the garden and had great sprays of the purple flowers [lilacs] in our hands and stuck in the children's hats, and when the Yankees rode away and the excitement subsided we were still holding the tossing, fragrant plumes. This is the third time these same two wretches have been plundering out here."[71]

It was no surprise but a great disappointment to masters and mistresses that enslaved workers fled when they got the chance. Stone's family had depended for generations on slavery, but she recognized the chinks in the armor: "Negroes on our place were protected from cruelty and well cared for; they were generally given Saturday evening and had plenty to eat and comfortable clothes. Still there were abuses impossible to prevent." And in the great southern tradition of "blame the neighbors,"

Stone suggests that these cruelties blighted "other" plantations—she'd heard "tales that would make one's blood run cold." She condemned herself and fellow slaveholders: "And yet we were powerless to help. Always I felt the moral guilt of it, felt how impossible it must be for an owner of slaves to win his way into Heaven."[72] Kate expressed empathy for the slaves' situation and even suggested that if she were in the same boat, she would be inclined to escape as well. Yet racism and resentment abounded, in Stone's and other women's wartime memoirs.

By the spring of 1863, no longer willing to withstand the increasing hazards, Stone's family felt it was time to decamp: "We have wakened three mornings to the booming of cannon and have gone to sleep to the same music, but we have not heard what they are doing."[73] The family headed west by boat and on horseback, beyond the bayou to Tyler, Texas, nearly three hundred miles away. This refugee resettlement was harsh, as the family felt unwelcome in their temporary home. Like many displaced aristocrats, they believed they were subjected to envy and prejudice.[74] Anchored on the far shores of the Confederacy, Stone mourned her younger brother Walter, who died a little over four months after enlistment, before he ever saw combat. The Stones felt robbed by war's relentless demands and forfeits.

When news of the Confederate surrender at Appomattox trickled its way westward, Kate felt doubly defeated and in May 1865 bemoaned: "The best and bravest of the South sacrificed—and for nothing. Yes, worse than nothing."[75] Her return to Brokenburn was forlorn: "It does not seem the same place. The bare echoing rooms, the neglect and defacement of all." By September 1868, after three years of sporadic entries, she closed her journal with, "So this is the end—shall I ever care to write again?"[76] Stone would remain a loyal Louisianan, marrying a Confederate veteran and moving to Tallulah to give birth to four children.[77] Even as a loyal member of the UDC, though, she raged against the war: "To me, it is all Murder. Let historians extol blood shedding; it is woman's place to abhor it."[78]

Louisiana women were eloquent in expressing opinions and observations, but women from nearly every state in the Confederacy contributed powerful chronicles of war. The private writings of planter-class women were suffused with regret, condemning the secessionist experiment.

This culture of complaint was most often kept under wraps, in favor of a female literature of exalting the war, and so this propagandistic payback is at times anachronistic to decode. Decorated war hero and former South Carolina senator, ex-Confederate general M. C. Butler proclaimed, "Do the annals of any country or of any period furnish higher proofs of self-sacrificing courage, self-abnegation and more steadfast devotion than was exercised by Southern women during the whole progress of our desperate struggle?" He went on to call the sufferings of men "mild inconveniences when compared with the anguish of soul suffered by the women at home." In front of an audience of CSA veterans in 1888, Butler reminded the soldiers of the "surpassing heroism" of Confederate women.[79] The hyperbolic glorification of female valor has been an article of Confederate faith that has only recently faced scrutiny.[80]

Certainly, referring to the damage done to a generation of southern men as a "mild inconvenience" is more than a slightly exaggerated understatement. It is a boast, a braggadocio, an example of the distorted lens of memory and the crazy quilt of neo-Confederate rhetoric. The press that exulted in Confederate women's sacrifice, the politicians that praised intrepid females during the 1860s, and the memoirists who enshrined and embellished female wartime heroism all contributed to a marathon campaign to sanctify the Confederate cause. The dawning of surrender evolved into a permanent noon of defeat. Neo-Confederates—stripped literally of uniforms and metaphorically of their kingdoms—sought to recreate lost splendor, particularly through elevating women back onto pedestals. This enshrinement involved much rhetoric and reason to believe that, once again, white women might symbolically uplift a civilization under attack.

The role of Queen of the Lost Cause was a sweepstakes for which several ambitious women competed. Some were cast in the role without auditioning, which was the case with Winnie Davis, known as the "Daughter of the Confederacy." Jefferson Davis's wife Varina had passed on this star turn, having enough to do with taking care of the fallen leader, trying to secure property and tranquility, getting her husband out of jail, then out of exile, and holding her family together in the months and years following Appomattox.[81] Yet her youngest daughter had been a prominent feature and symbol of the Confederate First Family since before she was born. Young Varina arrived in June 1864, shortly after her brother Joseph Davis, only five at the time, fell to his death at the Confederate White House on April 30.

The accidental death of the Davises' bright, healthy child sent ripples of sympathy across the city, across the Confederacy, and even into the North. His funeral became a public event as nearly a thousand Virginia children wound up the hill to Hollywood Cemetery for the burial. While the president and his pregnant wife stood witness, each child dropped onto the plot a bunch of spring flowers or a green spray, which became a mass of white flowers. Davis looked older than his fifty-five years, and one attendee was afterward haunted by Varina's "mournful, dark eyes."[82]

Many of the mourners were struck by the cloaked figure of the First Lady, burying one child while pregnant with another. Davis's biographer commented, "Richmond had no remembrance of a more moving funeral."[83] The daughter, born just one year before the Confederate surrender, embodied so many hopes and dreams for her parents. But Winnie struggled to fulfil her parents' wishes, and following education and travel abroad, she returned to their home in Mississippi.[84]

As she came of age, she became a favorite of veteran's organizations. She and her father frequently made public appearances, and they were often met by cheering crowds, until she ran afoul of her southern public in 1887 when she fell in love with a northerner, the grandson of an abolitionist. Her parents forced her to break off the engagement in 1889, and she never married. She died at the age of thirty-four and was given a military funeral because of her "service to the Confederacy." Davis was certainly a princess in the royal Confederate court, but she was unable to inherit the throne. Indeed, the title was one that needed to be earned by a combination of factors, including the ability to sway the public with the pomp and circumstance of a fallen nation. Turning defeat into a badge of honor was a requisite.

The Davis family as "fallen royalty" was a sentiment swept away by the advent of the twentieth century, when a set of determined former Confederate women began to compete for the hearts and minds of their fellow countrywomen. They recast the American Civil War as a morality play, with southern white women in leading roles and the Lost Cause as heroic. One of the most active candidates for a crown was born Sallie Ann Corbell in 1843. (She would knock a few years off her age when she found herself in the spotlight as a public figure in later life, and call herself "LaSalle.") When she married her dashing cavalier, George W. Pickett, in September 1863, his career was already on the decline, and he would be removed from command just a few days before Appomattox. His liberty was threatened by an impending government investigation of the hanging of federal soldiers in Kinston, North Carolina, in February 1864. Some wanted to charge Pickett with war crimes, so the former general took his wife and young son to Canada, where several communities of Confederate exiles relocated. Resettled in Montreal, Sallie taught French and piano, but times were hard, and the young matron was forced to sell her jewelry to help keep the family afloat. In Canada, she gave birth to a second son. General Grant intervened in Pickett's case, and he was able to return home to Virginia. Pickett obtained his pardon in 1874, but shortly thereafter, Sallie lost her seven-year-old son David Corbell Pickett. Her husband died the next year.

After Pickett's death in 1875, Sallie moved to Washington and became a government clerk in the Federal Pensions Office in order to support her surviving son.[85] Her grandfather Thomas Corbell had "believed in God, woman and blood."[86] His granddaughter launched a campaign to transform herself into a symbol of Lost Cause gentility. She dubbed herself a "child bride of the Confederacy," twenty years younger than her husband and barely out of her teens when they wed.

She painted herself as the wife of a hero, fallen on hard times. This portrait had wide appeal in an era when thousands of wives and children of veterans suffered in reduced circumstances. She took advantage of the end-of-century hunger for Confederate nostalgia. The celebration of "plantation epics" morphed into a craze for what I have discussed elsewhere as "Confederate porn," whites writing in blackface.[87] With the success of Joel Chandler Harris's Uncle Remus and Thomas Nelson Page's Marse Chan, LaSalle Corbell Pickett saw a bandwagon and hopped on it.[88] Beginning in 1900, she published a series of volumes, including *Kunnoo Sperits and Others, Yule Log, Ebil Eye,* and *Jinny.*[89]

Her literary career was part of a two-pronged propaganda front. She took advantage of the fact that her husband's name was forever linked with July 3, 1863—the last day at the Battle of Gettysburg. Gen. Robert E. Lee had ordered his men to renew combat engagement and to make a vainglorious march across an open field. Gen. James Longstreet was reluctantly put in command. Pickett was one of the three major generals who led this Confederate advance, yet his name is the one attached to the doomed attack, which was afterward designated "Pickett's Charge," despite Pickett's strenuous objections. Controversy surrounded the event: How had Pickett survived when three brigadier generals and fifteen officers fell? In 1888, W. R. Brand wrote about the event's legacy: "[It] had its place in books treating of the war, but has been more written about in newspapers and magazines than any event in American history. Some of these accounts, bordering on the hysterical, are simply silly. Some are false in statement. Some are false in inference. All in some respects are untrue."[90]

Frank Moore's record of the rebellion included an unflattering account of Pickett, in which a General Graham suggested "that Pickett himself was not in [the charge]. He describes him as a coarse, brutal fellow, and says he treated him with the greatest inhumanity after the battle, whilst wounded and a prisoner in his hands."[91]

Sallie Pickett devoted no small measure of her energy to rebranding her husband's name and took it upon herself to fashion a favorable historical account, *Pickett and His Men,* published in 1899. She might have rested on her laurels, but publishers pressured her to come up with more, and so she did. On the fiftieth anniversary of Pickett's Charge, his widow edited a volume entitled, *The Heart of a Soldier: As Revealed in the Intimate Letters of Genl. George E. Pickett* (1913). Her descriptions always provided a nostalgic account, with countless embellishments, praising Pickett as having "the greatest capacity for happiness and such dauntless courage and self-control that, to all appearances, he could as cheerfully and buoyantly steer his way over the angry, menacing, tumultuous surges of life as over the waves that glide in tranquil smoothness and sparkle in the sunlight of a calm, clear sky." The letters were not as florid, but they were just as self-serving.[92]

It took almost another half century for historians to conclude that these letters were such a compromised source as to be unreliable. Gary Gallagher has written convincingly about the passages that La Salle Pickett clearly cribbed from Walter Harrison's 1870 work *Pickett's Men; A Fragment of War History.* Not only did she shift from valorization to plagiarism, but there is further evidence that she stooped to fabricating correspondence—inventing letters from her husband and even from Abraham Lincoln.[93] Pickett's wife took the opportunity to blur the lines between fact and fiction, between literary license and outright invention—and to profit from her deceit. As Lesley Gordon has pointed out, these letters have been cited repeatedly by scholars, used in Michael Shaara's Pulitzer Prize–winning novel *The Killer Angels* (1974), and quoted by Ken Burns in his documentary *The Civil War* (1990).

Pickett was one of the first prominent women apologists who unabashedly promoted Confederate glory (and her husband's reputation), ignoring any matters conflicting with her personal vision or Lost Cause agendas. Liberating themselves from the weight and bother of evidence, this generation of neo-Confederate fabulists dominated at the turn of the twentieth century. Still, they believed they had their work cut out for them. They could not ignore history but rather intended to reinvent it in their own images. From the catechism of the junior wing of the UDC, which taught white southern children about the "disregard on the part of the States of the North for the rights of the Southern or slaveholding states," to the annual petitions to abolish Lincoln's birthday as a holiday, the twentieth-century neo-Confederates had an overflowing agenda.[94]

While men and women, North and South, might disagree violently over the contested terrain of the past, white supremacy—the most prominent feature of Confederate heritage— increasingly knit together former enemies. At the fiftieth anniversary of Gettysburg, the first southerner to be elected president since before the Civil War, Woodrow Wilson, proclaimed an abiding reconciliation. He pronounced at the battlefield reunion: "We have found one another again as brothers and comrades in arms, enemies no longer, generous friends rather, our battles long past, the quarrel forgotten—except that we shall not forget the splendid valor."[95] Promoting white supremacy and Confederate memorialization continued the hydra-headed project of this so-called southern heritage.

Few women took on the task of rewriting histories, except for *their own*. The publishers were eager to slake the public's hunger for memoirs, reminiscences and published letters, diaries and journals, creating a veritable cottage industry.[96] This bustling project of reinvention, re-fashioning, and re-creation lured many ladies into a frenzy of hope. One Confederate scribbler—a courtier at Davis's presidential palace—tried for some time to spin her reminiscences into gold. She wrestled with her manuscript, scrambling to revise and polish her wartime jottings. She tried her hand at magazine fiction but only sold one story and earned a pittance. That ten dollars seems to have been the only money she realized from her writing during her entire lifetime. Today, she remains the *most cited* Civil War diarist, with nearly a dozen editions of her work in print—the incomparable Mary Boykin Chesnut.

She witnessed the rise and fall of the Confederacy, tracing the inevitable trajectory of decline in gory detail. When her project finally appeared in print, her prose kept readers hanging on—even though we all know what's going to happen in the end. Chesnut's vivacity transforms her account into a page-turner. "We try our soldiers to see if they are hot enough before we enlist them. If, when water is thrown on them they do not sizz, they won't do; their patriotism is too cool."[97] The snap, crackle, and pop of Chesnut's brisk observations fascinate, despite exhibiting the same delusional lapses prevalent in the work of many of her sister scribblers, including Augusta Evans Wilson. Chesnut's writing appeals to modern readers for what it attempts to disguise as well as for what it reveals. Again and again, scholars dissect Mary Chesnut, not just to pick over her bones but to extract her very marrow. Recent brilliant interrogations include Julia Stern's in *Mary Chesnut's Civil War Epic* (2009)—an excavation—and Thavolia Glymph's "African-American Women in the Literary Imagination of Mary Boykin Chesnut" (2000)—a meditation.

Beginning with the 1905 appearance of her Civil War chronicle, Chesnut won widespread critical attention. She was born Mary Boykin Miller in 1823 on her grandparents' plantation, Mount Pleasant, in the Santee region of South Carolina. She enjoyed a privileged childhood as the daughter of a prominent southern statesman, Stephen Decatur Miller, who served first as governor of South Carolina, then won a seat in the U.S. Senate. During adolescence, Mary was courted by a bright young politician from Camden, James Chesnut Jr., who later assumed the Senate seat her father had held.

Like her mother before her, Mary wed at the age of seventeen— marrying in 1840 into the Chesnut family, whose fortune was derived from slaveholding. She concentrated her ambitions within the confines of her marriage, devoting herself to her husband's career during his life-time and to his legacy until her death in 1886. The state's political circles were dynastic and internecine, and her husband's position provided the couple with an entrée into Jefferson Davis's inner circle. Mary and her husband had unfettered access to the great events of the day—knowing everyone and hearing everything.

Therefore, the intrigue of Richmond's palace politics was interspersed with Chesnut's reflections on the events of the day. Her diary show-cased her talents, and she left her account laid out for close friends to read, sharing anecdotes as well as the sad record of mounting deaths and military reports. The surrender and subsequent events in South Carolina and throughout the South proved distracting and dispiriting to Chesnut. Following war's end, her husband escaped the scaffold and avoided imprisonment, despite his prominent position within the Rebel administration. Chesnut counted her blessings, but debt and worries piled up. Like the fictional Scarlett O'Hara, Chesnut rallied her family and household to withstand the ordeals of Reconstruction.

The realities of war and its consequences became unbearable, and Chesnut turned her hand to fiction. She tried to incorporate some of the ideas stemming from times she spent struggling with insomnia. For example, on New Year's Eve in 1863, she "did not sleep a wink. Like a fool I passed my whole life in review, and bitter memories maddened me quite. Then came a happy thought. I mapped out a story of the war . . . and the filling out of the skeleton was the best way to put myself to sleep."[98] When she wasn't coming up with clever plots in the night, Chesnut mulled over how she might blend together her notebooks of wartime scribbles into a publishable narrative.

She renewed her commitment to the project and vowed at the end of the 1870s finally to finish her autobiography. Mary began to embellish her scribbles—transforming as she transcribed. As she reshaped her journal, intellect and imagination met at center stage. She blended memories with hindsight to heighten the drama, massaging for effect.[99] The bedeviled author spent her later years wrestling with the manuscript, a burden she found increasingly unmanageable. She prayed she could write her way out of the hardscrabble life to which postwar poverty condemned her, especially with the death of her husband in 1885. She had begun her renovations by transcribing scraps and scribbles into forty-four notebooks and fifteen pads. She then rewrote, recalled, and recast events, assembling her jumble of palimpsests, which she hoped to mesh into a grandiloquent epic. The mosaic of memories, regrets, and glorification was in a constant state of flux. Her manuscript was suffused with popular motifs present in most epics—homecoming and hospitality—and she self-consciously invoked the ancients, whom she had read and continued to revere.

During her two main periods of intensive revising (in the late 1870s and, again, in the 1880s), Chesnut grappled with her dilemma. How might she turn observations into grand saga? In her final months of work, she interleaved amplifications into the original text, amending to make herself look prescient. One entry, allegedly penned in December 1860, hinted at future events: "I had better take my last look at this beautiful place, Combahee. It is on the coast, open to gunboats."[100] The Combahee River raid in June 1863 was followed shortly by the fall of Vicksburg and Lee's retreat from Gettysburg.

This would signal to South Carolinians the tilt of wartime victories in the North's favor—even as die-hard Rebels, Mary Chesnut included, valiantly tried to stave off defeat. Chesnut's warning that the Combahee region would be prey to gunboats was a *fake* harbinger. We know from comparative analysis of her copybooks that Chesnut made insertions—after the fact—to heighten drama within her narrative. She also sought to enhance a reader's appreciation of her intuitive skills. She tried to seamlessly fold retrospective commentaries into her wartime chronicle.

One of the author's frequent visitors during her days in Confederate Richmond was Louisa Wigfall [Wright], whose own memoir, *A Southern*

*Girl in '61,* appeared in 1905. Chesnut biographer Elisabeth Muhlenfeld points out that this memoirist praised her rival generously: "Mrs.
Chesnut was one of the most brilliant women of her time and as warm-
hearted as clever."[101] However, fire more than warmth and tartness more
than sweetness contributed to the popularity of Chesnut's writing. She
derided Rebel generals, as when she complained in November 1863:
"Misery is everywhere. Bragg is falling back before Grant. Longstreet, the
soldiers all call him Peter the Slow, is settled down before Knoxville."[102]
Or she might take a sharp jab at an African American servant and the
Yankees he ran off with: "Minus his fine watch and chain, Eben returned
a sadder and wiser man. He was soon in his shirt-sleeves, whistling at
his knife-board . . . 'I thought may be better stay with ole marster that
give me the watch and not go with them that stole it.'"[103]

She quite often braided together her contempt for African Americans
and northerners: "The Yankees, since the war has begun, have discovered
it is to free the slaves that they are fighting. So their cause is noble . . . we
bear the ban of slavery; they get all the money. Cotton pays everybody
who handles it, sells it, manufactures it, but rarely pays the man who
grows it. Second hand the Yankee received the wages of slavery. They
grew rich. We grew poor."[104]

She laced her put-downs with humor, but she could be snide when on
the offensive. On May 15, 1862, Gen. Benjamin Butler, the Union commander
of occupied New Orleans, issued his infamous General Order Number 28,
warning southern females to be respectful of the Union soldiers on the
street or face the consequences. Chesnut railed, "This hideous cross-eyed
beast orders his men to treat the ladies of New Orleans as women of the
town—to punish them, he says, for their insolence."[105]

Chesnut bumped up against the stringent rules imposed on women
in her own era. But by the time her volume appeared—nearly fifty years
after the war and twenty years after her own death—Chesnut's insights
seemed much more in tune with the era in which she was published. She
prided herself on being ladylike but recognized the limitations, and she
openly admired women who chafed at the bridle, like her South Carolina
comrade Louisa McCord: "She has the intellect of a man and the perse-
verance and endurance of a woman."[106]

Chesnut spoke her mind with an abandon that was reckless by nineteenth-century standards; she even made fun of this trait, confessing in the third person, "For once in her life, Mrs. Chesnut held her tongue."[107] Her bluntness reflects ferocious wit, as when she suggested that Byron might have been "a trying lover; like talking to a man looking in the glass at himself." She carped about the foreign press: "Those Englishmen come, somebody says, with three P's—pen, paper, prejudices." She encountered a woman who blamed South Carolina's "mischief" for causing the war. Chesnut let this insult pass, as the woman "told me she was a successful writer in the magazines of the day, but when I found she used 'incredible' for 'incredulous,' . . . I left her incredible and I remained incredulous."[108]

At the war's beginning, Chesnut described domestic routines alongside war news. She painted cozy pictures of dozing on the sofa, listening to the scratches of her husband's pen as he worked well past midnight. She would often come home by herself from a party—her excessive socializing was a source of friction between the couple. One evening after returning home from being out late, she "put on my dressing-gown and scrambled some eggs, etc. there on our own fire. And with our feet on the fender and the small supper table between us, we enjoyed the supper and glorious gossip."[109] These intimate details, as much as her political perspicacity, contributed to the book's popular appeal.

In their introduction to the first edition of her published manuscript, Isabella Martin and Myrta Lockett Avary reinforced the image of Chesnut as a "woman of society in the best sense."[110] In postwar South Carolina, whether bartering for food or reduced to wearing tattered gowns, Chesnut maintained her dignity. These genteel lady editors employed redaction to protect the privacy of those discussed indiscreetly; dashes and initials replaced many full names. Her editors would also reword the description of a woman from "ugly as sin" to "she was not pretty." They tried to tone down Chesnut's abrasive edges, although her voice could not be muted.

Racial strife was bubbling below the surface, often flaring up dramatically in the South; Chesnut's views raised eyebrows, if not hackles. Many of her comments about slavery were out of step with neo-Confederate ideology: "But what do you say to this—to a magnate who runs a hideous black harem with its consequences, under the same roof with his lovely white wife and his beautiful and accomplished daughters? He holds his head high and poses as the model of all human virtues to these poor women whom God and the laws have given him. You see Mrs. Stowe did not hit the sorest spot. She makes Legree a bachelor."[111]

This was a *searing* indictment, contrary to the lockstep of Lost Cause ideology. Confederate partisans in the postwar era actually suggested that "mulattoes" were a product of Union soldiers' illicit liaisons with African American freedwomen. They proclaimed that mixed-race offspring were rare before the war but could be blamed on Yankee licentiousness. This flew in the face of evidence that most light-skinned black Southerners traced their lineage back to southern slaveholding white men mixing with "colored concubines." Again, neo-Confederates brushed aside facts in favor of promulgating "truth" in order to counter Yankee falsehoods.

Chesnut viewed sex—the category and the act—as signifiers within her world. She liked to stir things up. Although she might include jottings about light-hearted aspects of the "battle between the sexes," her journal more often provided sharp and bitter commentary about gender divides. She knew that women, white and black, were expected to endure circumscribed lives, obedient to the patriarchal order. While men preached a doctrine of their own infallibility, Chesnut was quick to bring up male foibles and shortcomings.

Chesnut seemed to espouse some strain of "magnolia feminism," a precursor of "second sex" sensibility. She offered the tart observation that her husband had "been so nice this winter; so reasonable and considerate"—but then adds, "that is, for a man."[112] As Mary Wollstonecraft once warned, irony was the only weapon women might wield effectively. Even as a woman born into an aristocratic family and given the best education money could buy, Mary knew that her days of intellectual freedom were numbered; her wedding day would fix her fate.

When she married, she did not take on the role of plantation mistress, nor even mistress in her own household. Mary Chesnut was forced— as was the custom of the country—to live with her in-laws until her husband might inherit his own property or afford a separate estate.

Chesnut's duty was to become pregnant, to "be fruitful and multiply." Though the couple was, by all appearances, in love when they married, there is no evidence that she ever conceived—the record is unclear. In any case, Chesnut never carried a child to term, and she wrote poignantly about her status. The hope of becoming a mother had been extinguished by the time the Chesnuts became a power couple within the Confederacy. Setting aside any personal grief, childlessness caused social stigma.

Infertility was little understood, and women were designated as barren when couples failed to reproduce. James Chesnut Sr. expressed his fears that the Chesnut bloodline would be extinguished and salted the wound when, in front of his daughter-in-law, he confided to his own wife: "You must feel that you have not been useless in your day and generation. You have now twenty-seven great-grandchildren.'"[113] Chesnut lashed back in private, hinting that the colonel failed to mention his own mixed-race children in this calculation of progeny. She was sour and unforgiving on such matters.

Chesnut confessed she suffered "reproach among women" because females, too, had "contempt for a childless wife."[114] This was a lifelong cross for her to bear. In 1883, she confided to Varina Davis: "You should thank God for your young immortals—I have nothing but Polish chickens—and Jersey calves."[115] Although denied motherhood, Chesnut remained invested in her role as model matron, devoted wife, and southern lady. When she and her husband finally secured their own townhouse in Camden, she delighted in arranging her own décor and ruling her own roost. Without a bustling nursery, Chesnut turned to a gaggle of nephews and nieces to keep herself entertained. Society and family members reminded her that these substitutes could not take the place of flesh and blood heirs, and she found life in South Carolina considerably stifling.

When the couple moved to the District of Columbia following James Chesnut's election to the U.S. Senate in 1858, Mary finally found a more fulfilling role, one at which she could excel: political society hostess. She took seriously the task of filling her salon with witty conversationalists, inviting glittering visitors to her well-appointed dining table. She found politicians eager to share tales from behind closed doors, and she elevated entertaining in her home into an art form. Just as she was poised to reign supreme in Washington society, secessionist politics intervened. James Chesnut resigned his Senate seat and pledged his commitment to the cause of secession and Confederate independence.

Far from disappointed, Mary Chesnut was energized by the exciting prospect of a new capital, a new nation. In a taunt she surely later repented, Chesnut urged southern men to fight instead of talk. She prodded her husband to shift out of the wings and onto center stage during these tumultuous times. As political developments escalated, she schemed alongside her spouse, vying for advancement. He was first an aide to Gen. P. G. T. Beauregard, and served at Fort Sumter and Bull Run. Next, much to Mary's liking, he was promoted brigadier general and appointed an aide to Jefferson Davis. Mary had accompanied her husband to the first Confederate capital, Montgomery, but then relocated to Richmond, eventually outmaneuvering her rivals and winning over Davis's wife, Varina. The first lady of the Confederacy appeared aloof to many but clearly warmed up to Mary Chesnut, and this friendship put the enterprising Mrs. Chesnut right where she wanted to be. Wartime Richmond provided her with a new, more enticing environment.

Again, her intellect and humor served her well. She used Shakespeare's Hamlet to complain about the North's attempt to subdue the South: "We want to separate from them; to be rid of the Yankees forever at any price. And they hate us so, and would clasp us, or grapple us, as Polonius has it, to their bosoms, 'with hooks of steel.' We were an 'unwilling bride.'"

In her confessional writings during wartime, Chesnut might stray into heresy and make inappropriate commentaries on race and sex. She at times compared the plight of slaves with that of women: "You know how women sell themselves and are sold in marriage from queens downward eh? You know what the Bible says about slavery and marriage; poor women! Poor slaves!"[116]

But Chesnut was a woman with the common prejudices of her era, and her writing reflected the racial biases of her region and class. Her racism was in lockstep with the white majority of the South and with the nation as a whole. Her impassioned opinions concerning slavery have fascinated readers, and her use of masks and racialized imagery provides for intriguing interpretive insights.[117] Blacks make frequent appearances in Chesnut's writing and provide the vehicle for one of her most subtle manipulations, as she employs ventriloquism to afford blacks a voice—literally or figuratively putting words in their mouths. This kind of literary blackface is something I describe in *Tara Revisited* as "Confederate porn." Chesnut accused others of wearing a mask, when it was her own use of this metaphor that underscored the ambiguity of who was maintaining the masquerade.

Whether she was consciously inventing dialogue (perhaps as creatively as Mrs. Pickett did when she provided readers with her dead husband's wartime letters) or misremembering exchanges, Chesnut dotted her manuscript with vivid commentaries about African American characters and experience. She used black voices to reinforce her own prejudices about wicked Yankees and virtuous white southerners. She promoted tales of interracial fealty and boasted that her household maid Ellen hid diamonds from the Yankees, then returned these precious jewels to her mistress "as if they had been garden peas."[118] The reported benevolence of masters and fidelity of black dependents were meant to demonstrate slavery's positive aspects; thus, Chesnut remained a cheerleader for her class and Lost Cause propaganda.

Harriet Beecher Stowe was a favorite target for Chesnut's wrath. She believed her own cast of characters should replace the stereotyped caricatures of *Uncle Tom's Cabin*. Slavery was justifiable in Chesnut's estimation, due to black inferiority and their dependence on whites.[119] She dissembled wildly on a whole range of issues and incidents involving blacks, and her journal recounted one particular event that Chesnut found deeply troubling. In September 1861, her cousin Betsey Witherspoon was found dead in her bed. The first edition of Chesnut's published writings reported that her cousin died in her sleep, but the editors conveniently omitted the fact that authorities later discovered that Witherspoon had been smothered with a pillow, murdered by her slaves. This instance of slave treachery and betrayal haunted Chesnut. For the five months following this incident, Chesnut did not write in her journal, only resuming her chronicle in February 1862.

Even with the investigative work done by Elizabeth Muhlenfeld, Julia Stern, C. Vann Woodward, and others, the jumble of Chesnut's manuscript deceives: Is it a diary? A journal? A memoir? Reminiscences? What exactly can this visited and revisited manuscript be called? Each rendition of the published work is a form of hybrid. Scholar G. Thomas Couser calls it "a novelized chronicle in diary form." Whatever the label, her contradictions have kept scholars spellbound and readers absorbed with each rising generation, and her fame has survived well into the twenty-first century. She remains the creator of one woman's life and times, depicted in epic proportions.

But her writings might never have seen the light of day, if not for the band of sisters who supported and celebrated one another. In her final decade, from 1875 to 1885, Chesnut staved off her fears about an uncertain future. Her goal was to piece together the yellowing fragments of feelings and memory, carried with her from her war years. Perhaps the layers of meanings were too fluid to fix on the page. The more and more she wrote, perhaps the less secure she felt. All that she had invested in this project could not be packed into a single volume—which she feared might be viewed as flawed and as fading as its author. In the end, Chesnut failed to complete the project before her untimely death, leaving her magnum opus unfinished.

Mary Chesnut's failure to publish in her lifetime has almost always been addressed as some sort of tragedy—which of course it was *monetarily*. In other ways, it offers us an added opportunity to appreciate and understand white women's Confederate consciousness. Her diary's survival and publication was part of the collective work of nineteenth-century southern white women to preserve and promote their sisters who suffered and died too soon—before their stories were shared and praises might be sung.

The midwives of Chesnut's manuscript—the faded, crumbling concoction of pages that became one of the most treasured records of the Civil War—remain unheralded. Chesnut was wise enough to entrust her unfinished manuscript to her good friend Isabella D. Martin, a South Carolina educator, a literary woman, and a longtime friend from wartime years. Martin remained a faithful supporter over the decades. Aware that her faith and passion might not be enough to see the project through, Chesnut willed her notebooks to Martin sometime in July 1885—six months after James Chesnut died and a little over a year before her own passing.

It took another twenty years before Martin shared the manuscript with Myrta Lockett Avary, whose 1903 memoir *A Virginia Girl in the Civil War* reinforced her literary fame. Avary discussed the project with her publisher, D. Appleton and Company, and Appleton editor Francis Whiting Halsey signed up Chesnut's manuscript, with Martin and Avary as coeditors.

Halsey insisted that his "lady editors" pan for the gold, sifting out treasure from the mountains of material left behind. Halsey played a large role, as the editorial troika culled roughly 130,000 words from the more than a million Chesnut left behind. Martin and Avary saw themselves as Praetorian Guard, ready to polish the halo as well as the pedestal. Their introduction promised readers that Chesnut's chronicle was "radiant," a work representing the "luminous mind, the unconquered soul of the woman who wrote it."[120]

Their volume aimed for maximum public effect, appearing first in installments in the *Saturday Evening Post,* as "A Diary from Dixie." With this popular serialization in 1905, Mary Chesnut was ready for her close-up. Since the first publication of her autobiographical writings, Chesnut's reputation has experienced ups and downs. Her volume was kept in print and then was reinterpreted by novelist Ben Ames Williams in his 1949 edition, also entitled *Diary From Dixie*. Next, C. Vann Woodward assembled a team of experts and researchers in the 1970s to get to the bottom of the complex cluster of incomplete, doctored, and censored manuscripts. In 1981, Woodward published his compilation of manuscripts as *Mary Chesnut's Civil War* and won the Pulitzer Prize.[121]

As in her own day, Mary Chesnut attracted male admirers, causing many literary men of the twentieth century to lavish praise: Douglas Southall Freeman called her book "the most famous war-diary of a Southern woman." Louis D. Rubin Jr. declared she had produced "by all odds the best of all Civil War memoirs, and one of the most remarkable eyewitness accounts to emerge from that or any other war." Finally, none other than William Styron proclaimed Chesnut the author of "a great epic drama of our greatest national tragedy."[122] In 1962, Edmund Wilson elevated Chesnut with his magisterial *Patriotic Gore: Studies of the Literature of the American Civil War*. Wilson's affair with Edna St. Vincent Millay and his failed marriage to Mary McCarthy might demonstrate his proclivity for "difficult" women, but with his approbation, he remains in good company. A parade of modern scholars has succumbed to Chesnut's charisma.

The American Civil War became the impetus for Chesnut's self-conscious embrace of a supporting role for herself within her new country, at the critical moment of its creation. Denied a biological child, perhaps she decided to make the Confederacy in its infancy her very precious project. But with Confederate defeat, she recognized that her enthusiasm had been misplaced, and she was forced to confront the demise of a dream. She resisted the realization that, for her own former slaves and the millions of emancipated African Americans who surrounded her, the Confederate surrender would usher in the dawn of a new era. Mary Chesnut was propelled down her long, lonely road homeward, "condemned to Camden."

For the next half century, leading up to the bicentennial of the Civil War, she may not lose her title as Queen Bee of the Confederacy, but it is certainly up for reinterpretation.[123] The Confederacy and its symbols will continue to be demystified—and definitely diminished.

The band of sisters who forged bonds to hold fast during what they believed would be the darkest of days might not be erased from the historical landscape but given a new gloss. Their memories, defeats, and dreams live on within the meditations of their hearts translated into words on the page. We might deny them their truths, as dissemblance rather than self-reflection saturates even the most confessional of Confederate women's testimonials. The blood of the lash could not be whitewashed away by even the most eloquent of memoirists, and yet the band of sisters would die trying.

# TWO

~~~~~

# Impermissible Patriots

I am neither a man nor born in this country, but my heritage and my sex
are no impediment to patriotism. . . . What a woman may do if she dares
and dares to do greatly.

—LORETA JANETA VELAZQUEZ, *THE WOMAN IN BATTLE* (1876)

Once upon a time, the stories didn't always begin with "once upon a
time." Instead, the stories might begin "our people." The stories might
be handed down from one generation to the next, and would generally
involve hardship and challenge, passion and patriotism, and they always
touched on memories of a homeland. At times, there would be dramatic
interruptions in a peaceable kingdom—with *wars* the most likely diver-
sions. Wars would catapult and cleave and cause realignments, in the
name of duty to the state. Citizens might say: I will take my stand and
face death with pride, fulfilling my obligation to a higher power and
my nation, and if fate decides I should join my ancestors in permanent
slumber, so be it.

So, young and old, male and female learned that war was part of the
cycle of life—a way of keeping faith with the past. Southern families beguiled by telling stories of warriors, fierce and proud—some mounting a
barricade, plumed hats and all, while others were traced to battles across
the sea, fighting off European invaders to evade enslavement. Warriors,
placing forebears first, were willing to risk the family bloodline to defeat
an enemy. Descendants, even immediate offspring, took a backseat to the

ancients from whom the race sprang. As children gathered around southern hearthsides to hear boasts of valor, even random listeners could discern that while men might be expected to roam, women were anchored at home. This was the order of things.

Yet, there were those who resisted—particularly emboldened girls who felt the need to uncouple themselves from the harsh dictates of gender convention. With the Confederacy under construction and under siege, there was opportunity for white women to be part of the grander scheme of things. Those determined to defy the dictates of their day—to participate or contribute outside the boundaries of female propriety—generally went unheralded. Or, if they made their mark, their defiance rather than their accomplishments was noted, and thus they became *impermissible* patriots.

The most impermissible of patriots were women who disguised themselves as men to serve their country. Those who served in male disguise to accompany sweethearts or husbands to war were perhaps less transgressive than those who sought male valor or identified as men. Even so, all who challenged gender norms were perceived as a danger. This threat had to be dealt with immediately upon discovery; women who pretended to be men were sharply and severely rebuked, if not punished.

The most impermissible of patriots, the most extraordinary and exceptional of soldiers, was Loreta Janeta Velazquez. Very few historians, even those within the Civil War community, invoke her name. Perhaps even fewer have read her extraordinary autobiography: *The Woman in Battle.* The first edition of her memoir, published in 1876 in Richmond, included an impossibly convoluted "tell-all" subtitle of the type so popular in the nineteenth century: *A Narrative of the Exploits, Adventures, and Travels of Madame Loreta Janeta Velazquez, Otherwise Known as Lieutenant Harry T. Buford, Confederate States Army. In Which Is Given Full Descriptions of the Numerous Battles in which She Participated as a Confederate Officer; of Her Perilous Performances as a Spy, as a Bearer of Despatches, as a Secret-Service Agent, and as a Blockade-Runner; of Her Adventures Behind the Scenes at Washington, including the Bond Swindle; of her Career as a Bounty and Substitute Broker in New York; of Her Travels in Europe and South America; Her Mining Adventures on the Pacific Slope;*

*Her Residence among the Mormons; Her Love Affairs, Courtships, Marriages, &c., &c.*

I came across Velazquez several decades ago and have been pleased to learn more about her from exceptional colleagues, including Maria Agui Carter, whose award-winning film *Rebel!* is a creative and elegaic meditation on this remarkable figure. Elizabeth Leonard has been heroic in lifting Velazquez from the footnotes. Leonard explains the levels of subversiveness Velazquez's character embodies when she suggests that Velazquez was not just "a woman soldier" but that she was an Hispanic woman in "white brothers' war." And finally, DeAnne Blanton and Lauren Cook's remarkable *They Fought Like Demons: Women Soldiers in the Civil War* offers Velazquez in historical context.[1]

Born in Cuba but raised in New Orleans, Velazquez was sent to live from an early age with relatives in Louisiana so she might be trained to be a proper lady. Her transgressions began in childhood; she was not just a tomboy or a youth who had taken a fancy to wearing male clothing. She longed to break free of her assigned gender role. Velazquez reported from an early age that she was ready to burst out of the confines of nineteenth-century imagination. Her adventures are so wide and deep that they almost defy definition, and some have charged they *are* unbelievable.[2]

But she laid out her life story in a sprawling epic, and most of what we know about Velazquez's life and career, especially her role in the American Civil War, derives from her own memoir. The motivation for this narrative of her unorthodox wartime experience and her extremely complicated personal ambitions remains unknown. The market for wartime memoir prompted many to write for money, and Velazquez may have had this in mind when she prepared her autobiography.

Like many veterans, Velazquez may have felt adrift, and perhaps she was willing to embellish her identity for recognition, as well as compensation. She was perhaps down on her luck, and looking back at wartime as the period when she was most full of a sense of purpose, perhaps fueled by adrenaline as well as patriotism. We do know that her book certainly stirred up interest and trouble for its author. She was a woman who defied so many conventions that it's is difficult to know where to begin.

First and foremost, her memoirs demonstrate that she was daunted by the challenge of impersonation: "I must learn to act, to talk, to almost think like a man."[3] She found this no easy task, confessing, "I am compelled to sink my sex entirely. The least inadvertence can be my ruin."[4] Velazquez had been an extraordinary child, and although she declared that she loved her mother, she confided, "it was my father I wished to emulate—and I would hang on every detail as he told me of his adventures." She grew up with a fertile imagination and dreamt of her future by looking to the past: "Joan of Arc, the Maid of Orleans, was my favorite heroine, an example of what a woman may do if she only dares, and dares to do greatly." So "daring" was embedded into the psyche of this rebellious youth, who had no hesitation in saying, "I wish I had been born a man instead of a woman." She then added, "But, being a woman, I have always tried to make the best of it."[5] It is fairly hard to imagine what "making the best of it meant" during this period.

"I wish I had been born a man" is a fairly common refrain in the memoirs of Confederate women of the period, particularly young women.[6] Many took men to task and complained that they, too, wished they could serve or that they wished women rather than men were in charge. But only a few dozen southern women testified as to why they hoped to pursue such an extreme path as to serve in the military in disguise. Wartime allowed emboldened women an opportunity to make good on their desires. And even *fewer* left any record of their time in uniform, making Velazquez's account all the more valuable.

Today, Velazquez might be viewed as someone whose identity reached outside the boundaries of normative heterosexuality. Perhaps she might be considered to have been experiencing gender dysphoria, as her distress as a young woman led her into dramatic and transgressive responses, particularly for her era. Velazquez might fall within the category transgender, but to label her thus would be highly speculative.

Although she clearly expressed conflicts over her identity and never found any community within which to share her aberrant sensibilities, there is also plenty of evidence that she enjoyed aspects of femininity within her culture. For example, if she did identify as a man and was struggling with her female body, then she might have done herself quite a complicated disservice by taking a husband three or four times. (The record is murky as to how many times Velazquez succumbed to convention and married her lovers.)

Equally compelling, her identity might have been detached from her pursuit of marital status. Women in nineteenth-century America were warned repeatedly that they needed protection and that the only path to personal fulfilment was by acquiring a husband and creating a family. Females were assigned value in terms of their running a household and producing a family, and little else. Male superiority and female inferiority was a given.

Within Hispanic culture, the stakes were even higher. In both the Anglo and Hispanic cases, females were designated the lesser sex. But the honor culture and reinforcement of patriarchal dictates was even more robust for women in non-Anglo communities. Removed from her parents at the age of seven, Velazquez was sent to live with a family role model who would nurture and educate her ward. This aunt was an old New Orleans Creole, who imposed severe strictures, as Velazquez complained: "Everyone was determined I should be a proper lady." She added rebelliously: "Except me."[7]

Racism gave the youthful Velazquez quite a shock when she landed in Louisiana. Hispanics of any nationality were culturally stereotyped as savage, barbarous, inferior. Velazquez could not understand this stark differentiation, a departure from what she had known in her homeland. Here she was in a port city of the Caribbean, being reclassified as a woman of color, as someone who was not "white." New Orleans, in particular, was a complicated laboratory for understanding the social constructions of race during the antebellum era.

While being educated by the Sisters of Charity, Velazquez was given a strict Catholic upbringing. Concerned about their daughter's unorthodoxy, her parents arranged for her to marry the son of a Spanish family when she was in her early teens. Velazquez found herself at odds with this Old World custom in her New World setting. The pupils in her academy, "when they found that I was betrothed without my own consent, were at a great deal of pains to inform me that this was a free country, and that one of the chief blessings of living in a free country was, that a girl could not be compelled to marry any particular man if she did not choose to do so."[8]

Velazquez demonstrated her first and most determined streak of independence by falling in love with a non-Hispanic who is identified in her memoir as a Protestant Texan named William. In 1856, she defiantly married this Anglo, which deeply offended her family. The scandal created a permanent rupture between Velazquez and her father.

When her husband was sent on an expedition to Utah in 1857, Velazquez had just given birth to their first child and could not accompany him. Family happiness was marred again when the army dispatched her husband to Indian Territory. By this time, she had two offspring—a mother of two before the age of eighteen. Sadly, when she gave birth to a third child, her baby died. It was a difficult challenge for the young mother to maintain her equilibrium, burying a baby without her husband there. And what followed was even more crippling, as Velazquez became inconsolable when her two remaining children succumbed to fever.

When Texas voted to secede in February 1861, her husband resigned his commission (at her urging) and elected to train recruits for the Confederate Army in Pensacola. When he died shortly thereafter, Velazquez became despondent, bemoaning, "I must have occupation for mind and body, such as will prevent me from dwelling on my grief."[9] She had given up family to create a family—she had lost her children, trusting them to a loving God, but now she had been deprived of her only remaining support—her husband—who died in the service of his country. Consumed by grief, the young widow decided to take up arms herself.

Civil War armies were very different from our modern military; soldiers, for example, lived outside almost all the time. Also, most soldiers were very young, so it was not unusual for a soldier to have a high-pitched voice or to not yet have sprouted a beard. A woman might find it easy to resemble a beardless youth and to disguise her sex by wearing baggy clothes. Velazquez had experimented with male clothing when she was younger, and so she was revisiting familiar territory.

In the nineteenth century, notions about gender were so clearly associated with particular forms of dress that someone in pants was immediately assigned a male identity. It simply did not compute that a person in male clothing might be anything but a man. Prohibitions were very strong about gender and dress. By 1900, nearly three dozen cities and twenty-one states had passed laws against cross-dressing. Yet, Velazquez knew that donning a costume was a key part of her mission and confessed: "I am ready to play my part in a great drama. It is strangely simple to arraign myself in my soldier's uniform and no one thinks to stop me."[10]

She was committed to "showing I am as good a warrior as any man."[11] However, because "battles are few and far between," she found "camp life most oppressive."[12] There were other disillusionments. She fantasized about "the most stupendous adventures. The story of the siege of New Orleans fired my imagination." And yet Velazquez reported, in the army, "self-seeking is more common than patriotism . . . and in camp, a spirit of petty jealousy is even more prevalent than it is at a girl's boarding school."[13] She was baptized by fire when she participated in combat at Woodsonville (December 1861), the Battle of Fort Donelson (February 1862), and the Battle of Shiloh (April 1862): "I fire my revolver at another officer—who is in the act of jumping into the river. I see him spring into the air, and fall; and turn my head away, shuddering at what I have done."[14] This participation in battle and the trauma of murdering another person, Velazquez confessed in her memoir, provided turning points.

In order to strengthen her identity as Lt. Henry Buford, a Confederate officer, she had purchased a slave named Bob. Bob was a good cover, but after the Battle of Shiloh, he escaped to Union lines to secure his freedom. Velazquez, as Buford, did not pursue him, but she found that her disguise was becoming more rather than less difficult. She was wounded and left for dead, then put on a train with corpses. Hurt, she had to avoid medical attention—despite the pain—lest her sex be discovered. The disillusionment continued, as she learned, "To be a second Joan of Arc is a girlish fancy, which my experiences as a soldier dissipated forever."[15] Velazquez was much more transformed by participating in wartime slaughter than she was by pretending to be a male soldier.

When she was unmasked and thrown in jail, a Virginia newspaper reported, "An investigation into the suspicious character of the young man revealed . . . in fact 'he' was a woman."[16] Velazquez was released to Confederate general John H. Winder and took on an even more dangerous assignment as a Confederate agent, suggesting that, as a woman, she could "often do things that a man cannot."[17] She moved into a new phase of service: "I pass through the lines in the north and the south, inventing my past as needed. I associate with traitors and make men betray the cause to which they are bound." In the memoir, she reports that she fell in love with another soldier, married him, and that her new husband (Thomas DeCaulp) was tragically killed; the record suggests De-Caulp deserted and enlisted with the federal army. Some hints indicate that Velazquez may have switched sides as well, to spy for the Union. She was able to confess: "It will be a decade before I am able to make sense of all I have witnessed," and it indeed was a decade before her memoir appeared.[18]

In 1875, a handbill circulated, announcing *The Woman In Battle* and promoting it as if it were the greatest Civil War book ever written. There is every reason to believe that Velazquez was willing to make her autobiography "the greatest" by embellishing incidents. Self-promoting aggrandizements were common during this era, if not de rigueur. Her contemporary critics as well as current dissenters suggest that Velazquez's style includes fabrications that go beyond mere embellishments. One contemporary historian has suggested that the book represents full-scale invention, whole-cloth fraud.

---

Vicki Ruiz has said that Velazquez risked much by publishing the book under her own name and that we must recognize how important the act of writing was for Velazquez. Perhaps besides being an impermissible patriot she was an outsider to the coterie of Confederate women memoirists, her work falling well beyond the boundaries of sisterhood scribblers.

Today we can appreciate that Velazquez achieved more as an author than as a soldier. Her book is full of sharp and tart insights, and she shared her struggles as a writer: "It has taken years to write the book and find a publisher. At last in 1876, the book is ready for release. Those who knew me and fought alongside me are more than happy to vouch for me. I am eager to reveal my experiences to the world and share a woman's perspective on war." Indeed, Velazquez seeks to place her own experience alongside those of other women warriors, as she makes clear in a lengthy historical aside:

> Far back in the early days of the Hebrew commonwealth Deborah rallied the despairing warriors of Israel, and led them to victory. Semiramis, the Queen of the Assyrians, commanded her armies in person. Tomyris, the Scythian queen, after the defeat of the army under the command of her son, Spargopises, took the field in person, and outgeneralling the Persian king, Cyrus, routed his vastly outnumbering forces with great slaughter, the king himself being among the slain. Boadicea, the British queen, resisted the Roman legions to the last, and fought the invaders with fury when not a man could be found to lead the islanders to battle. Bona Lombardi, an Italian peasant girl, fought in male attire by the side of her noble husband, Brunaro, on more than one hotly contested field; and on two occasions, when he had been taken prisoner and placed in close confinement, she effected his release by her skill and valor.[19]

She is sensitive to those who would discredit female military achievement with objections devolving into attacks on women's virtue. She is particularly concerned about validating her own experiences and motives, testifying in the book's opening pages: "How well I did play my part, happily does not depend upon my own testimony alone, for some of the most distinguished officers of the Confederate army, and many equally distinguished civilians, can and will testify to the truthfulness of the story I am about to relate, and to the unblemished character I bore while in the Confederate service."[20]

At the time her memoir appeared, many ex-Confederates were invested in the project of promoting the Lost Cause. One former military leader, Jubal Early, was extremely canny and understood how print might influence interpretations of historical events, which is why he rejected whatever interfered with the glorification of Confederacy.[21] As a gatekeeper, Early gave Velazquez a short, brutish review: "I came across Madame Velazquez's book, entitled *Woman in Battle,* and gave it a cursory examination, from which I was satisfied that the writer of that book, whether man or a woman, had never had the adventures therein narrated . . . and I have expressed the same opinion to several presses in the city." After trashing her book, Early goes after the author: "Madame Velazquez might have been a follower of one or the other army in some capacity, but the book cannot be a truthful narrative of the adventures of an army person." Velazquez's shock and dismay was exacerbated by the fact that she had respected Early. She declared that they had fought together at Bull Run, and she was extremely disturbed by this deeply personal attack and insisted upon confronting him. Although Early did not want to meet with her, she forced an encounter (at the hotel where he resided) to ask him to retract his libel. He never did, and his label of "fraud" has echoed down through the decades.

Hinting that she might have been a "camp follower" was a low blow, but perhaps the worst is yet to come. Another notable scholar of the Civil War seems much invested in the topic; William C. (Jack) Davis, is assembling a volume that disputes Velazquez's claims concerning her entire life. He proclaims that she was not Cuban born and that little else is true in her autobiographical account of her life, and he intends to expose her as a fraud. In a June 2015 interview, Davis confided that he thinks of her as the "Confederate Kardashian."[22] He further suggests: "In fact she was a lifelong fraud, almost certainly a prostitute in New Orleans when young, and after the war a compulsive confidence artist of amazing ambition, including trying to capitalize a railroad across Mexico for $50 million. . . . She genuinely was a pioneer among female confidence artists."[23] Davis delivers an extremely backhanded compliment, and whether his admiration for her is genuine or feigned, Davis, like Early, maintains that Velazquez was a prostitute. (In private correspondence, Early also slandered Velazquez by saying that her book is surely the work of a northerner, which was to him the most devastating charge he could level.)[24]

Alongside discrediting Velazquez as a soldier and chronicler of her wartime service, both Davis and Early seem confident in labelling her as sexually compromised, claiming that she must have been a "camp follower" or a woman paid for sex. Historians may seek to verify or discredit these charges and to debate the evidence of Velazquez's claims, but what is quite clear is that these particular male authorities—born over a century apart—feel quite confident in taking this tactic to undermine a woman who was so audacious as to take a defiant position and then to advertise her perversion. Even in the name of Confederate glory, such female audacity is off-limits—and impermissible patriotism can be brushed aside by calling a woman who exhibits it a whore. Such tactics were even more common in wartime, when lines of male authority were disrupted.[25]

During the rise of social disruptions, evidence indicates that women who wanted (proverbially) to loosen the corsets (or even abandon them altogether) temporarily could shed suffocating sex role stereotyping. The record abounds with girls and women defying rules of conduct as they adapted to "wartime exigencies." With this kind of wartime dislocation, younger women might wonder if they too could make their mark? Yet, southern gender rebels even more than their northern counterpart met with stiff resistance once men came marching home.

White southern men were charged with keeping ladies on the pedestal, and that pedestal came equipped with a lock and key. Patriarchs remained guardians of the race, their name, and their family legacies. That wasn't always so good, and yet it was the way it had always been, and perhaps might ever more be? Men would be men, and women must be whatever men required—carrying out the wishes of the patriarchy, Even in the face of relentless slaughter—in the name of protecting family honor—which could and did ensue, women would use handkerchiefs to wave men off to battle and also to wipe away tears when corpses were returned for burial. Many old southern bloodlines were snuffed out when war left thousands upon thousands dead.

Johnny donned a uniform to defend his people on the field of battle. His sister might have similar desires, but her moments riding astride or even bareback—abandoning the principles of domestic womanliness—only temporarily suspended propriety. Her duty was to put on the good front of welcoming home losers as winners. Patriotism after the war demanded that women's hearts be purged of pride in their own accomplishment, to place male glory in the spotlight. All was focused on restoration to status quo antebellum.

If a girl continued pushing against the fences, she might earn the reputation of "tomboy." As she approached adolescence, the white southern daughter must turn her back on roughhousing, lest it be mistaken for immodesty. She must trade in any masculine airs in favor of crinolines and bows.[26] What might have been acceptable in terms of an interest in fauna must be tamed into cultivating flora, with virginity on the verge. There was a time and place for everything within the rural South, and the female world of ritual was a key component of white planters' much-exalted "way of life." Young women were expected to set aside childish things, in favor of childbearing themselves. They were expected to produce the next generation as soon as they shed their own baby fat. And the fruit they bore would perpetuate dynastic prerogatives.

Missteps were met with instantaneous consequences, as society could slam the door, leaving an errant female out in the cold.[27] Yet war offered temptations to stray beyond the boundaries, perhaps even undetected. Young girls might have viewed wartime as an opportunity for masquerade—as if playfully assuming a disguise. We do not know how many women took advantage of loosened constraints to take on masculine roles or even to don costumes to impersonate men, but some individuals left behind traces of personal rebellions.

Slaveholders of old liked to hearken back to the Bible, to the days of Adam and Eve. Perhaps they could not even conceive of the likes of Lilith. I certainly did not learn in Baptist Bible camp about the figure of *Lilith,* Adam's first wife . . . made of dust like Adam. Her refusal to recognize the superiority of her husband caused her to be cast out of Eden. She chose to live with the devil and beget demons, only sleeping with humans infrequently—making contact as a succubus. Lilith's "visits" are a folk explanation for "nocturnal emissions"—whereby a primeval woman returns to drain men as they sleep.[28] So the woman who refuses to accept her own inferiority, who defies the patriarch, gets banished and transformed into an enchantress, a seductress. Naturally, society suggested congress with such a woman led to danger, damage, or even death.

These lessons were not lost on impressionable young white girls lined up in Sunday morning pews. One false step did not necessarily indict two people, because it was always the *woman* at fault, even if it was the fall of man. Punishment might be so swift and terrible that it took many a woman by surprise. Females were kept in check by a ward system, and white women's chastity was a community concern, policed by males and females alike. Once they reached menses, females were expected to attract parentally approved beaux, make an advantageous match, and continue the bloodline. Even though Velazquez's schoolmates encouraged her to seek her own match, southern parents expected filial piety and obedience. This custom of the country was intended to keep females pure within a culture with a sexual double standard bubbling just beneath the surface. Racial transgressions were doubly dangerous and threatened to upend society—even after slavery's demise, white patriarchs harped on racial purity and female chastity. Domesticity and piety must rock the cradle rather than any boat.[29]

Girls with intellectual interests were discouraged and would be sent spinning on their way. Alas, spinsters who remained too long unattached might lose a seat at the table—forfeit their chance. As dependents with no hearths of their own, they might be designated as extra hands in a family member's household. They might suit as a second wife, a companion to an aunt, or helpmeet for a married sister. These rigid, permanent patterns rarely fluctuated. But if and when they did relax, there was almost always a *permissible* excuse—like war. During wartime, marriages were organized with what would have been deemed indecent haste in any other circumstance; engagements and honeymoons were cut short. With so many young men dashing off to enlist, young girls found options fleeting.

Gender was not something that you could slip in and out of easily within the antebellum era, within a plantation society. Gender bending—what little there was—mostly took place within a more urban, fluid society. The institution of plantation slavery emphasized the need for circumscribing. Even within antebellum southern cities, escorts, badges, and papers were required to maintain proprietary control.

Women in the North were equally bound by domestic divides but seemed more adept at negotiating for themselves. They might test the waters as public scolds, inching forward from perches as the keepers of a family conscience. Thus, increasingly within nineteenth-century America, women confined to the domestic sphere might extend their reach, pushing outward in concentric circles to redefine their roles within the comforting space of "domestic housekeeping." These women who pushed outside the bounds of gender convention were undermining the status quo, risking reputations, but inched outward by invoking the language of domesticity—they only wanted to insure moral order be maintained in the untamed public sphere.

Civil War–era women reformers of all stripes have been showcased in a series of scholarly tomes, including Lori D. Ginzberg's *Women and the Work of Benevolence: Morality, Politics, and Class in the Nineteenth-Century United States* (1990), Sylvia D. Hoffert's *When Hens Crow: The Woman's Rights Movement in Antebellum America* (1995), Rebecca Edwards, *Angels in the Machinery: Gender in American Party Politics from the Civil War to the Progressive Era* (1997), and Julie Roy Jeffrey's *The Great Silent Army of Abolitionism: Ordinary Women in the Antislavery Movement* (1998).[30] We learn from these and many other general works on American women that ordinary females were nearly always northern—and almost always white.

Most Civil War historians highlight sectionalism, and increasingly American women's historians more vigorously have introduced issues of region and race into gender analyses. Judith Geisberg's *Civil War Sisterhood: The U.S. Sanitary Commission and Women's Politics in Transition* (2005) and Anne M. Boylan's *The Origins of Women's Activism: New York and Boston, 1797–1840* (2002) are exemplary studies with regionalism appropriately contextualized. In both Nina Silber's *Daughters of the Union: Northern Women Fight the Civil War* (2010) and Jeanie Attie's *Patriotic Toil: Northern Women and the American Civil War* (1998), northern urban women are identified as forerunners of reform, pathbreakers on behalf of women's expanding sphere.

This is not to say that there were no southern women undertaking the important domestic tasks associated with war work, but women in the 1861 Rebellion rose to the occasion in alternate ways, for example, with artistic flourish. Confederate women, in particular, left behind a vibrant legacy in cloth—quilts and handkerchiefs, crewelwork and embroidery, bandages and yarn. Women's contribution to material culture during the Civil War has been on lavish display in wonderful museum exhibits during the sesquicentennial and in new volumes published over the past few years—in particular, *Homefront and Battlefield: Quilts and Contexts in the Civil War,* a richly illustrated catalogue to a traveling exhibit curated at the American Textile History Museum in Lowell, Massachusetts. Curators Madelyn Shaw and Lynn Zacek-Bassett heroically tracked down a rich array of decorative objects.[31] Where possible, they incorporated contemporary images—daguerreotypes, lithographs, and paintings—to illuminate the era. Their detective work—the stories behind the stories—is laced together with sketches of marvelous resources dug out of collections.

We are treated to the history behind the beautifully appliquéd chintz quilt lovingly crafted for George Washington Gordon, who joined the Confederate army in 1862. His family kept the quilt for his return, but it remained in storage following Gordon's 1865 death.[32] The fascinating Reunion Ribbon Quilt (1881) commemorating an Indiana regiment, as well as the epic tale contained in Lucinda Ward Honstain's "Reconciliation Quilt" (1867), offer powerful testimony to this artistic form. Historians need to re-craft (literally) as well as rewrite stories reflecting women's wartime experience.[33]

Confederate women patriotically pledged their time and energy to undertake traditional feminine domestic roles. As a poem in the *Charleston Courier* instructed:

> Fold away all your bright tinted-dresses
> Turn the key on your jewels today.
> And the wealth of your tendril-like tresses
> Braid back, in a serious way.
> No more trifling in the boudoir or bower,
> But come with your soul in your faces,
> To meet the stern needs of the hour![34]

At one point during the war, the stern needs of the hour included donating silk petticoats to the Confederate command. During the Seven Days battles in 1862, the federals launched balloons that allowed them critical advantage; Confederate general James Longstreet sent out an urgent message to the countryside to try to obtain enough material to construct a Rebel balloon. The resulting patchwork contraption was dubbed by Longstreet "the last silk dress in the Confederacy." Unfortunately, it was captured by the Union navy on a steamer that went aground in the James River, but its creation shows the way in which chivalric tradition both exalted and exploited women's talents.

Confederate ladies decked out their menfolk with frock coats and sashes, epaulets and gaiters, and supplied soldiers with a portable "housewife" (a compact cloth kit equipped with thread, needle, buttons, and perhaps scissors). Men on the march might survive by keeping their equipment and weapons in working order, but blankets, uniforms, and homemade items kept men in balance as the war dragged on and on. Personalized items handmade by loved ones were treasures for many enlisted men; sentimental items with a practical purpose served as reminders of home. Tobacco pouches—some with elaborate fringe and decoration—became a favored token of remembrance for departing soldiers.

Sisters, mothers, and daughters might patriotically trill "Song of the Shirt" as they worked on military piecework—just as men sang their marching songs. Ladies' sewing circles gathered to stitch havelocks (hats with protective cloth hanging down from the back and sides), roll lint for bandages, or perform any number of useful tasks associated with women's work. Simple tasks were transformed by wartime exigency. The most mundane of tasks, like darning socks, were now war work. Hundreds of thousands of women pushed themselves along this path, with male approval. Over the course of the conflict, women's *permissible patriotism* was encouraged, heralding "needles as daggers."

Women might be drafted into using their needles in other spheres as well—encouraged to take on nursing and medical duties in their own homes, in makeshift hospitals, or, as the war wore on, in hospitals. Before 1861, no lady would minister to men who were not family members. After the war broke out, when ill and injured soldiers poured into communities, ladies found themselves in a dilemma: Should they refuse to be compromised by proximity to men who were not their kin or should they offer up their hands to serve the Confederate wounded? What might happen if their guards were let down?[35]

Many prominent, aristocratic women volunteered to undertake the drudgery of nursing—duties that were usually the domain of men in the public sphere and of ethnic workers or enslaved servants in the private sphere. The only white women who possessed any previous medical experience were sisters in religious orders, such as those described by Virginia Gould in "'Oh, I Pass Everywhere': Catholic Nuns in the Gulf South During the Civil War."[36] Nuns were the only group who had managed hospital care as a component of their female duty. Eventually, scores of well-born Confederate women—Catholic, Protestant, and Jewish—would not only serve but recruit others to follow their example, demonstrating the domino effect of war.

Prohibitions faded erratically, but generally hospital work came under the heading of acceptable service for women and even provided *paid* work for widows later in the war. Cornelia Kincaid wrote to a friend about her mother's decision to work as a matron in a Rome, Georgia, hospital, explaining apologetically to a friend, "very nice ladies have gone in as matrons."[37]

Some ladies safeguarded their reputations by taking African American attendants with them into the wards. Black and white women both found employment in the most famous hospital in the Confederacy, Robertson Hospital in Richmond (named after the judge who was persuaded to donate his home to the Cause). When the war broke out, Sally Tomkins was an unmarried twenty-eight year old from a prosperous family in the Confederate capital. After the Battle of Bull Run, she recognized the need for immediate action and set about organizing wards in Robertson's home. This hospital would treat over twelve hundred wounded during its four years of operation, and President Jefferson Davis awarded Tompkins a military commission as captain (which she accepted) and a salary (which she refused). Her devotion to the soldiers in her charge made her a legendary Confederate patriot.[38]

But southern women, like their northern counterparts, learned that sometimes the medical care needed to go to the wounded men on the battlefield, rather than expecting the soldiers to survive until transport to a hospital. Juliet Hopkins, wife of the former chief justice of Alabama, performed such heroic service that she was nicknamed "the angel of the Confederacy." Hopkins was at the Battle of Seven Pines and went out onto the battlefield to tend the injured; while on the field, she was wounded in the leg and walked with a limp the rest of her life.[39] Ella King Newsom, widow of an Arkansas planter, trained as a nurse in Memphis in 1861 before going into the field with Gen. Albert Sidney Johnston in Kentucky. She moved to where she was needed, serving in hospitals in Bowling Green, Nashville, Chattanooga, and finally Atlanta.[40]

Both Scottish-born Kate Cumming (who worked in hospitals in Georgia) and Phoebe Yates Levy Pember (who served at the Chimborazo Hospital on the outskirts of Richmond) left memoirs detailing their wartime nursing careers.[41] Pember was a widow (like Newsom), while Cumming remained single throughout the war.

Much more commonly, women refugees and women left behind might be drafted into providing care to ailing men in uniform. Wives following their husbands volunteered during trying times. Fannie Beers described how she was given a baptism by fire when half-dead Alabama troops were deposited in a warehouse in the Confederate capital, and she threw herself into nursing: "Four of our sick died that night. I had never in my life witnessed a death-scene before, and had to fight hard to keep down the emotion, which would have greatly impaired my usefulness."[42]

Another nurse, Selina Johnson, worked in a hospital after the second Battle of Bull Run and recalled the terrible ordeal of a patient's agony: "The last few days he lived, the only way he could get any relief from terrible pain was for someone to clasp around the leg with both hands as near where it was cut off as they could and while clasping it tight, press the flesh down over the end of the bone. It was very hard so we nurses took turns."[43] Confederate women pulled into this project of caring for soldiers might find themselves enduring exhausting ordeals even as men claimed they were weak and inferior. Indeed, by war's end, many women would rankle at the crippling stereotypes that held women back and, once they leapt over hurdles, those persistent prejudices that sought to diminish their accomplishments.

Naturally, those women who took on clandestine wartime roles as spies, scouts, and couriers might not expect their praises to be sung. They did not undertake vital but dangerous missions to become the center of attention but rather used the cloak of secrecy and the myths of female delicacy to advance the Confederate cause. Females who chose to defy the dictates of the era remain relatively unheralded heroines; discretion was a necessary virtue, and after the war, women might be excluded from tributes not just because of the secrecy surrounding their missions but because women would be compromised if such dealings were revealed. Ladies' reputations might be sullied permanently if involvements were acknowledged.

Clearly, there were scores of loyal Confederate women who gathered intelligence to convey vital information to military and political leaders. Those few who became celebrities for their exploits were special cases, and their celebrity came with a price. Spies were a colorful and exotic breed during the Civil War, and saboteurs and informants played a key role in several Confederate victories. The records from spy missions remain scarce, and it becomes difficult to disentangle fact from fiction, exploits from embellishments. The rise of the popularity of spy stories following the Civil War has also further complicated problems of authentication.

A New Orleans–born aspiring actress, Harriet Wood took the stage name of Pauline Cushman in the 1850s.[44] She then toured with a theater company during the war. While performing in Kentucky, she offered a toast to President Jefferson Davis, playing the part of a pro-South partisan. This was done to avert suspicions about her real agenda, working on behalf of the Union army. Ingratiating herself with Gen. William Rosecrans, she smuggled materials from inside Rebel tents into the hands of Yankee commanders. Clearly, she was able to infiltrate where many others had not succeeded. However, once caught, she was tried for her capital crime and given the death sentence by Confederate general Braxton Bragg. She was able to escape this fate and toured the North, embraced by enthusiastic audiences. Indeed, when she was in Manhattan, a crowd serenaded below her window. When Cushman appeared, she made brief remarks to the assembled: "I am no orator, and make no pretence to eloquence; but as our gallant Gen. GRANT, when called upon to make a speech, I can say, 'I can fight for my country.'"[45]

For her efforts, she was awarded the rank of major. Her exploits were not only intended to advance the federal cause but also to advance her own personal career. Cushman published her memoir in 1864, even before the war had ended: *The Romance of the Great Rebellion: The mysteries of the Secret Service: a genuine and faithful narrative of the thrilling adventures, daring . . . Union forces, of Miss Major Pauline Cushman.* As "Miss Major Cushman," she attracted celebrity and the patronage of none other than P. T. Barnum (who held the copyright to her memoir). As an actress in nineteenth-century America, Cushman was already compromised, as ladyhood was rarely associated with women in her profession (or women in any profession for that matter). (Her identity is further complicated by her mistaken inclusion in the Dover publication *Famous African American Women.*)[46]

Women smugglers were much more common than women spies, although there is evidence that these activities went hand in hand or under the umbrella of "Confederate agents." In 1859, when she was not yet twenty, Belle Edmondson's family relocated from Holly Springs, Mississippi, to Shelby County, Tennessee. When the war broke out, Belle was so eager to participate that she actively sought a role as a scout for Confederate officers. She was a favorite of those soldiers who appreciated her enthusiasm. She described her activities in a letter dated March 16, 1864:

> I began to fix my articles for smuggling, we made a balmoral of the Grey cloth for uniform, pinned the Hats to the inside of my hoops, tied the boots with a strong list, letting them fall directly in front, the cloth having monopolized the back & the Hats the side. All my letters, brass buttons, Money &c in my bosom. . . . Started to walk, impossible that, hailed a hack . . . rather suspicious of it, afraid of small pox. . . . Arrived at Pickets, no trouble at all—although I suffered horribly in anticipation of trouble.[47]

She was right to be nervous; her activities were eventually discovered, and after the federals issued a warrant for her arrest, she retreated back to Mississippi and waited out the war there.

Women passing through the pickets often hid valuables on their person. Mary Chesnut reported that bustles were suspect and false hair might be searched for papers.[48] A large number of women were involved in schemes to deliver medicine—prohibited by law—from beyond Confederate lines. A niece in the Blair family was caught trying to leave the

District of Columbia with one hundred ounces of quinine sewn into her skirt.[49] She was released just a short time after she had been thrown in jail, but authorities took very seriously the plots of women spies passing along intelligence and military secrets.

It was clear to both sides in the war's earliest weeks how important spying might become when Gen. P. G. T. Beauregard clobbered Union forces outside Washington at the First Battle of Bull Run in July 1861. Society hostess Rose Greenhow became a notorious Confederate agent in Washington and was credited with sending him vital information that helped him secure his victory. Rose O'Neale had been born in 1813 on a small plantation in Maryland, where her father's death threw Rose's mother and her three sisters into a precarious economic position. Rose and her sister Ellen moved out of the family household and in with their mother's sister in Washington, D.C. Both girls made advantageous matches: Ellen married Dolley Madison's nephew, and Rose married Robert Greenhow, a lawyer who worked at the State Department. The Greenhows had four daughters, and the family traveled in Mexico and California for Robert's work before his accidental death in San Francisco in 1854. Rose settled back in Washington and threw herself into raising her daughters and enjoying the parlor politics in the capital.

When the war broke out, although she had friends on both sides of the aisle, Greenhow favored the Confederacy, and her situation at the center of wartime Washington gave her a ringside seat to Union activities. As a popular hostess, she mixed with everyone in Washington, an access of which she took advantage. In July 1861, Rose Greenhow was able to send General Beauregard a message via her courier, Betty Duvall, who approached Gen. Milledge Bonham at Fairfax County Courthouse, plucking a small package out of her hair to pass along to Beauregard. Though historians debate the significance of such messages, both Beauregard and Jefferson Davis thanked Greenhow for her contribution to the rout of the federal army at the creek near Bull Run, Virginia. Certainly, the federals feared leaks, and on August 23, 1861, put Greenhow and her young daughter Rose, under house arrest. Then, in January 1862, authorities sent her to the Old Capitol Prison, imprisoning her eight-year old daughter as well. In diva fashion, Greenhow took her maid along.

Such a public confinement appears to have been a risk that failed. Federals hoped to contain Greenhow's spy ring, but she was able to smuggle out information—and her missives reached a wide audience. She would wrap her daughter's rubber balls with messages and bounce them out of her cell to an agent in waiting. Her resourcefulness and rants frustrated her captors. Pressure built to release her, as she wrote stinging rebukes from her jail cell about Yankee depravity. Her goal was to generally promote havoc. She wrote about what she had endured when Yankees turned her home into a prison: Fort Greenhow, where she suffered the "total disregard of all the laws of decency. Every feeling of the woman had been shocked and outraged, and they now sought to act upon my nervous system, by dark insinuations and threats against my life and reputation."[50] And even worse, she and her child had been locked up in a federal facility, treated little better than common criminals.

She defied the authorities—including Secretary of State William Seward—who confronted her with charges of espionage. Greenhow retorted, "If Mr. Lincoln's friends will pour into my ear such important information, am I to be held responsible for all that?" Indeed, the authorities eventually thought it better to release her and deport her to Virginia, where she was given a hero's welcome. Mary Chesnut reported on June 6, 1862: "Mrs. Rose Greenhow is in Richmond. One half of the ungrateful Confederates say Seward sent her. My husband says the Confederacy owes her a debt it can never pay."[51] Greenhow took this good will and went on the road, showered with praise and feted wherever she went. President Davis invited her to be his goodwill ambassador and sent her to Europe to lobby on behalf of the Confederate government. He wanted her to be eyes and ears for his government, particularly in London.

Her memoir of her time in jail painted as bleak a portrait of the Yankees as she could. Abroad, she met with diplomats and financiers to try to advance southern independence and win friends for her new nation. Returning to the Confederacy in 1864 with important papers and gold, she drowned on October 1 off the North Carolina shore, trying to run the blockade. Greenhow was hailed as a "Martyr to the Cause" and given a hero's military funeral. Ann Blackman's vivid biography, *Wild Rose: Rose O'Neale Greenhow, Civil War Spy*, offers new and important information about Greenhow's life and career. The motives and machinations of this infamous Confederate spy continue to fascinate.

First and foremost, Greenhow's self-conscious role as a patriot and pathbreaker continues to provide fodder for intense debate. Greenhow was a staunch supporter of slaveholding and a Confederate partisan, which has resulted in neglect of her role as a pathbreaker for her gender. Her own Confederate sisters, who might have held her up as an icon, were suspicious of her character. She might have compromised herself with illicit relations (perhaps even before the war) and could not fulfill the requisite of being a paragon of virtue, a dictate every southern lady must at a minimum appear to maintain. While Confederate authorities might welcome any activities that helped them obtain intelligence from the enemy, they could not condone trading favors for information, which is what most males (and likely females) suspected of those well practiced in espionage.

Mary Chesnut and fellow Confederates sympathized when Greenhow revealed the deliberate and provocative "outrages" the federals imposed: "A woman of bad repute, known and recognised by several of the guard as such, having been seen in the streets of Chicago in the exercise of her vocation, calling herself Mrs. Onderdunk, was brought to my house, and placed in the chamber of my deceased child adjoining mine. For what object I know not, but this woman was allowed unrestricted intercourse with me, the order being given that our meals should be served to-gether."[52] Thus the "prostitution" card was played by women against other women, as well as by men against women, whatever their class.

Shortly after Greenhow's military funeral with honors, her Confederate heroism became tainted by suspicion that, in her zeal to serve, she had compromised her gender and her class. How had she coaxed information from such a wide range of Yankee contacts? What did she do to pry intelligence from Col. E. D. Keyes, a secretary to Winfield Scott? Furthermore, she was discredited during her own lifetime. Damning evidence was found in her home—a cache of intimate correspondence tied up in ribbons and hidden. These billets-doux from a married senator, Henry Wilson of Massachusetts (who would later serve as vice president under Ulysses S. Grant) were seized and disappeared into federal custody.

Perhaps concealed for the purposes of blackmailing, the letters indicated that Greenhow was a threat to Union security, as she might have inroads into federal powerbrokers. Her Mata Hari role—whispered about in Washington and a topic of speculation more widely—caused Greenhow to be ignored during the distribution of credit and glory afterward. Yet again, as she had learned as a girl in Maryland, the men may be fallen, but the women remain at fault.

More careful and intellectual attention to her memoir is warranted, even as propagandistic and self-serving as it appears—what memoirs aren't self-serving? Greenhow was carrying a copy of her reminiscences, with a note to her daughter, dated November 1863, when she drowned. The letter to young Rose read: "You have shared the hardships and indignity of my prison life, my darling; and suffered all that evil which a vulgar despotism could inflict. Let the memory of that period never pass from your mind."[53] Greenhow was perhaps well aware that she needed champions and provided instructions should she not survive her dangerous attempt to run the blockade, which indeed led to her death.

She might have worried what her reputation and legacy would be. Could she be remembered as a clever and resourceful provocateur, a woman who turned "Fort Greenhow" into a nerve center of Rebel resistance in the heart of wartime Washington. Furthermore, she seemed adept at inspiring others, such as Eugenia Phillips, the wife of a former Alabama congressman. Phillips had been charged with espionage and detained with Greenhow in Washington in 1861. She relocated to New Orleans and perhaps took the agitprop lessons from her sister spy along with her.

Phillips became one of the few females detained and exiled in the wake of Gen. Benjamin Butler's infamous "reign of terror" against the Rebel women of the town who defied federal authorities during the occupation. Butler had been no friend of emancipation when the war broke out yet became increasingly hostile to slaveholders as the war progressed. By the time he landed in New Orleans in April 1862, the general had zero tolerance for resistance from Rebels. He especially resented the way in which local ladies would withdraw from pews in church if a Union man chose to sit nearby or would depart from streetcars if a Yankee boarded. A local woman would gather up her skirts and desert the sidewalk rather than risk contamination by contact with any federal soldier. Such insults were annoying, but they did not draw any fire—until a white southern woman *spat* into the faces of two federal officers.[54]

As news of the incident circulated, Butler was furious. Could his men resist responding to such provocation? Shouldn't some appropriate measure be put in place to derail these outrages? Confederate diarist Julia Le Grand commented that "the *women only* do not seem afraid. They were all in favor of resistance."[55] Confederate female resistance took increasingly public and disruptive forms because women had little fear of retaliation.

All of New Orleans reeled when Butler issued his infamous General Order No. 28 on May 5, 1862: "As the officers and soldiers of the United States have been subject to repeated insults from the women (calling themselves ladies) of New Orleans, in return for the most scrupulous non-interference and courtesy on our part, it is ordered that hereafter when any female shall, by word, gesture or movement insult or show contempt for any officer or soldier of the United States, she shall be regarded and held liable to be treated as a woman of the town plying her avocation." All females in New Orleans who showed insulting behavior toward his men would be treated as "public women": arrested, booked, put in jail overnight, and "fined in front of a magistrate the next morning."[56]

By accusing southern ladies of being no ladies at all, Butler was trying to beat them at their own game. He suggested that their behavior dishonored southern civility and made them liable for their actions. The mayor complained that Butler's order provided a license for occupying soldiers to commit outrages—and the term *outrage* was loaded with sexual connotations. The female population was aghast, including Clara Solomon, a young white girl who confided to her diary that she would like for the women of her city to tie Butler up in ropes—or, better yet, sizzle him in a frying pan.[57]

Butler became the butt of rude jokes among the locals in New Orleans. His nickname became "Beast Butler." Allegedly, the prostitutes of New Orleans paid their own special tribute by pasting his portrait inside chamber pots.[58] He was reviled not just in Louisiana but also throughout the Confederacy. Mary Chesnut feared for her countrywomen at the mercy of such a "hideous cross-eyed beast."[59] Even Secretary of State Seward was unhappy with Butler's wording of the order. He regretted that "in the haste of composition, a phraseology which could be mistaken or perverted could be used."[60]

Seward was wrong to imagine Butler's "haste of composition," however. The order was discussed and dissected word by word before it was sent to the printer. A member of Butler's own staff, a Major Strong, raised objections to Butler's phrasing, wondering if "some of the troops may misunderstand." He was concerned what might happen if even one man "should act upon it in the wrong way." General Butler was resolute: "We are conquerors in a conquered city; we have respected every right, tried every means of conciliation, complied with every reasonable desire; and yet cannot walk the streets without being outraged and spit upon by green [young] girls."[61] And to Butler's credit, following the order, incidents of insult were precipitously reduced. A northern journalist crowed, "The morals and manners of no class of women in the world were ever so rapidly improved as have been those of the Secession women of New Orleans under the stern but *admirable regime* of General Butler."[62]

But one of the women who was arrested took a leaf from Rose Greenhow's playbook: Eugenia Phillips was insolent during an interview with a soldier after her detainment on June 30, 1862. She had already been charged with espionage in Washington the year before and had essentially been released on good behavior. With this second offense, she was branded a repeat offender and sent into exile. Union authorities transported her to Ship Island in the Gulf of Mexico, where she was confined to residence in a railroad car. This situation was considerably dangerous, as the island was a holding spot for yellow fever patients. Phillips reportedly told Butler, "It has one advantage over the city sir, you will not be there. It is fortunate that neither the fever nor General Butler is contagious." But during her ten-week incarceration, her bravado faltered. Her husband worked to free her from her vermin-infested confinement. She scribbled letters detailing the agony of her ordeal and publicizing Yankee horrors. Much of her correspondence mirrored the harsh sentiments and rhetorical flourish practiced by Rose Greenhow. When she finally was released, she fled the reach of the federals.[63]

Phillips was part of an elite group of Confederate women resisters—those few women acknowledged as Confederate partisans and heralded by their countrymen as notorious patriots. She and Greenhow left journals behind and perhaps they, as much as any Lost Cause authors, might be viewed as part of the venerated band of sisters.

However welcome these propagandists became, women's voices on the public platform were quite a shock to Confederate patriarchs. Yet they were in a bind, particularly when it came to Greenhow.[64] Despite her critical contributions, her defense of the realm, and her death in the service of her country, Greenhow's reputation was tinged with suspicion, the result of prejudice on the part of the United Daughters of the Confederacy and other organizations. Greenhow's methods were unorthodox, to say the least, and scandalous at best. The gossip with which her name became associated outweighed appreciation of the service she rendered. It was most likely women who put a damper on enthusiasm for elevating her to Confederate sainthood. She was not a saint, but she was a complex and dynamic example of Confederate patriotism.[65] She has been consigned to minor-league status within the southern women's history pantheon—perhaps, in the twenty-first century, because of her rabid proslavery support more than any other factor.

At the same time, such a fascinating career and compelling memoir calls attention to a woman who was unquestionably patriotic—but in such an *impermissible* manner that she is banished both by pro-Confederate and anti-Confederate schools of thought. Greenhow was surely one of the best-known impermissible patriots within the Confederate nation.

If Greenhow had any rival for the title of most infamous female spy for the Confederacy, it would certainly have to be agent, courier, spy, and promoter extraordinaire, Belle Boyd, who became famous during her exploits in the North, the South, and abroad. In February 1863, Margaret Johnson Erwin, deep in Mississippi, wrote enthusiastically: "the Union army has taken a woman named Belle Boyd, regarding her as a spy of considerable importance; I doubt that last most seriously. Yet I am glad to see women getting into this horrible political pudding. I hope that Miss—or Mrs.—Boyd gives them WHAT FOR and gets away with murder."[66]

Indeed, she already had "gotten away with murder." Boyd shot and killed a federal soldier at her parents' hotel on July 4, 1861. Following an investigation, Boyd eluded charges and remained free. This remarkable leniency became the norm for females charged with espionage or even the occasional murder. Women were rarely punished for their roles as traitors, and none were executed for war crimes, except Mary Surratt, convicted as a coconspirator in Lincoln's murder.

Belle Boyd's extraordinary coterie of soldier-suitors and use of her sex appeal in pursuit of extracting military intelligence highlights how some women manipulated gender conventions. In using her feminine wiles to advance political and military ends, much like Rose Greenhow, Boyd employed "women's weapons" but refused to play by society's elaborate rules. These Confederate adventuresses demonstrated that females could be both effective and, as one Union officer said of Boyd, "dangerous."[67]

This dangerous woman, born Maria Isabella Boyd in 1844, began her career at seventeen. She belonged to a family with staunch secessionist leanings; her father was a member of the Stonewall Brigade, and two uncles and a cousin were convicted of spying during the war. When federal soldiers occupied Falling Waters on July 2, 1861, near her home in Martinsburg, Virginia (later West Virginia), Boyd armed herself when Yankees invaded the town. When a drunken Union soldier behaved insultingly toward her mother, Boyd shot the man for his attack on the Confederate flag, his dishonoring of her mother, and general principle. She escaped punishment and was able to manipulate female stereotypes to her own ends, becoming an indispensible agent and courier, particularly reporting to Stonewall Jackson.

By nineteen, she had been imprisoned at the Old Capitol Jail in Washington. Despite capture, she was always returned home to civilian life, after promising to be good. Thus, with each catch and release, Boyd gained more and more confidence. She became bolder in carrying out her plots, and Jackson often wrote to thank her for her assistance. She treated her espionage career as a military assignment, wore a quasi uniform, and adhered to a strict code of conduct. It was her own invented code, which puzzled many of her benefactors. She was a woman, using her wiles, but also a soldier, with a distinctive style. The *New York Tribune* detailed her personal adornments: "a gold palmetto tree [pin] beneath her beautiful chin, a Rebel soldier's belt around her waist, and a velvet band across her forehead with the seven stars of the Confederacy shedding their pale light therefrom." In this dashing attire, she was variously described in the press as "La Belle Rebelle" and the "Amazon of Secessia."[68]

Sharon Kennedy-Nolle creatively suggests Boyd's hybridity: "Caught between two polarized nineteenth-century postures, Boyd embodies two narratives of patriotic service that were available during the war; the domestic drama of proper lady engaged in self-sacrifice, and a military drama of 'manly' self-assertion and courage." In a unique manner, Boyd was both a lady and a cross-dresser, or "*half-dressed* in each gender's vestments." Her appearance was a part of her allure, and one fellow prisoner described her through the bars: "a slight figure, in the freshest summer-toilette of cool pink muslin; close braids of dark hair shading clear, pale cheeks; eyes that were made to sparkle, though the look in them was very sad, and the languid bowing down of the small head told of something worse than weariness."[69]

She used her notoriety as a stepping-stone to a stage career, which led one scholar to speculate: "Was Belle Boyd actually a heroine or was she an imposter? Was she a 'good woman' of excellent lineage and education or was she an immoral, sordid and disloyal character of obscure origin and condition."[70] Clearly, she set her sights on a larger vocation when she landed in Europe in December 1863. She had gone there allegedly to regain her health but was sailing back to the States, when she was captured on the blockade-runner, the *Greyhound*. While detained on board, she conveniently fell in love with a federal naval officer, Samuel Hardinage, who let her slip away into Canada rather than be subjected to detainment, prosecution, and possible imprisonment. Later, Boyd and Hardinage met up in England and married. Hardinage returned to the United States, where he had been charged—quite understandably—with aiding and abetting the enemy. He was arrested upon his arrival but was released from prison, and later his whereabouts were unknown.

Boyd, back in England, claimed she was a pregnant widow in need of assistance. She gave birth to a daughter, published *Belle Boyd in Camp and Prison* (1865), and tried to support herself as a professional Lost Cause champion. Her book was a kind of parodic spy novel with a healthy dose of political propaganda. She recounts being asked by captors to take an oath of allegiance to the United States and says that she refused: "Sir, if it is a crime to love the South, its cause, and its President, then I am a criminal. I am in your power; do with me as you please."[71] She performed onstage, and her branding herself as the "Cleopatra of Secession" became critical to her overall strategy.

She returned to the States after the war, married two more husbands along the way, and was billed on her national tour as the "Siren of the Shenandoah." One of her greatest problems was impersonators, as one paper reported: "Belle Boyd, the Confederate Spy, who died recently at Plymouth, England, is living at Corsicana, Texas in easy circumstances. She is also living in a garrett [sic] in Baltimore, where she makes a scanty living by needlework, so the papers say. Belle is beating her Confederate record of being in two places at the same time."[72] In reality, she continued with her stage career for nearly two more decades and died in 1900 while on tour in Wisconsin, where she is buried.

Studying Boyd requires negotiating a thicket of confusion, with crumbs of deception sprinkled along the way. Her later life arouses curiosity: she was for a short time confined to an asylum, while pregnant. Can this indicate that she suffered from some kind of depression? Some papers referred to her as suffering from "insanity," always something I look upon skeptically in my line of biography.[73] Clearly, Boyd had a lively interest in the opposite sex, to the extent that she was called "crazy" when around army camps, which caused no end of derogatory sniping. Many other women in the Virginia valley region were involved in elaborate spy networks, but Boyd was the most notorious. She suggested, "all the mischief done to the Federal cause was laid to my charge; and it is with unfeigned joy and true pride I confess that the suspicions of the enemy were far from being unfounded."[74] When news of one of Boyd's arrests reached her, Lucy Buck, who also shuttled messages, confided to her diary about her fellow patriot: "I hope she has succeeded in making herself proficiently [sic] notorious now."[75]

But she was no fellow—she was a sister—and therefore many of her activities meant that her sex disqualified her reckless voluntary service, and her patriotism was impermissible.[76] At the same time, some admired this quality, and Boyd became a poster child for the Rebel spirit, celebrated in song and newspapers. As the *Knoxville Daily Register* applauded, "this fair and fearless Virginia heroine, whose daring defense of her father's house, when Charleston, Va., was first invaded by the Yankees and whose invaluable services in conveying information to our lines in spite of the espionage of the craven foe have won for her from the Northern press the title of the most courageous and dangerous of rebel female spies."[77]

Yet, all this transgressive behavior did not result in the dreaded *feminism* symbolized by the liberated women's rights advocates in the North—seeking women's ability to vote, demanding to keep their own wages, and other gross violations of laws of decency. Boyd proclaimed early in her memoir that she was *not* any "advocate of the woman's rights doctrine" because she "endeavored to avoid politics."[78] This was a peculiar statement from a woman who risked her life to advance the cause of the Rebellion.

Thus, male authorities *reluctantly* praised and endorsed Boyd's activities. A Confederate officer who had met her in Winchester in March 1862 later commented, "If necessity had required it, I believe she would have led the charge of Pickett's Division at Gettysburg without a tremor."[79] A southern Baptist minister summed up his divided feelings: "while I could not consent that *my* daughter should pursue such a life, I cannot help admiring the spirit of patriotism which seems to control her conduct."[80] Meanwhile, the Yankee press derided women spies, attacking she who would defy that which was "holiest."

As the war dragged on for months and years, many women were unhappy about their choices—or lack of choices. Some were angry that their husbands spent so much time away from the home they were allegedly fighting to protect.[81] Some younger women were disappointed that their circles of young male friends were dying in droves, leaving the southern landscape eerily empty. This emptiness could and did lead some intrepid women to strike out on their own, and again, perhaps only the upheaval of war could have prodded women into abandoning gender markers completely and disguising themselves as men.

We have no idea how many women served as soldiers during the American Civil War, but we have a fairly good *approximation* of those discovered, thanks to the historical detective work of DeAnne Blanton and Lauren Cook, in their extensive survey, *They Fought Like Demons: Women Soldiers in the American Civil War* (2002). Blanton and Cook have documented roughly 250 women who fought in the guise of men during the Civil War, an important corrective to Mary Livermore's guestimate (in her memoir) of four hundred—a number which stood for too long without interrogation.[82]

This topic continues to be incredibly controversial, despite the simple fact that there were women who defied conventions and for a variety of reasons attempted to serve in the military despite prohibitions. United States officials and experts even resorted to outright denial when in 1909 Ida Tarbell wrote to the adjutant general F. C. Ainsworth asking whether his department had "any record of the number of women who enlisted and served in the Civil War, or has it any record of any women who were in the service?" The response was prompt: "I have the honor to inform you that no official record has been found in the War Department showing specifically that any woman was ever enlisted in the military service of the United States as a member of any organization of the Regular or Volunteer Army at any time during the period of the civil war. It is possible, however, that there may have been a few instances of women having served as soldiers for a short time without their sex having been detected, but no record of such cases is known to exist in the official files."[83] This may have technically been true, but Ainsworth was clearly perpetuating a falsehood.

This official line has caused interpretive problems, as Blanton outlined in a 1993 article in *Prologue,* an official publication of the National Archives: "While references, usually in passing, are sometimes found, the assumption by many respected Civil War historians is that soldier-women were eccentric and their presence isolated. Textbooks hardly ever mention these women." Two leading Civil War scholars of the late twentieth century, Bell Wiley, the preeminent expert on the common soldier, and Mary Elizabeth Massey, author of a centenary study of American women and the war, provide examples. Wiley wrote at some length of "the gentler sex who disguised themselves and swapped brooms for muskets [and who] were able to sustain the deception for amazingly long periods of time." But he later refers to them, indirectly, as "freaks and distinct types." Massey erroneously asserted that "probably most of the women soldiers were prostitutes or concubines."[84]

This question of white southern women's transgressions during the midpoint of the nineteenth century is tied into a web of female historical questions and evidence too vast and dense to tackle as a whole. But tangential topics can help us understand historical forces at work during this period of erratic alignments and adjustments. There are literally scores of fascinating topics ripe for further exploration, and these meditations are meant to prompt change—both by marking some developments and graduating on to a new playing field of investigation.

One underexplored topic in need of an intervention is dress reform. American feminists challenged the restrictive clothing assigned them during the early republic, especially as radical women identified "femininity" as a stumbling block to both autonomy and equality. As Amelia Bloomer advocated—"women and men had equal claims to 'the enjoyment of all these rights which God and nature have bestowed upon the race.'" And thus, she wrote, "woman is entitled to the same means of enforcing those rights as man."[85] She joined with other nineteenth-century women's rights advocates in pushing for the vote.

But her unusual zeal for parity allowed her to see women's clothing as an impediment on the road to equality. Male reformer Gerrit Smith suggested that "changing woman's dress would transmute her in the eyes of men and prepare her for the 'battle of life.'" Bloomer and others advocated this transformation and supported adoption of "Turkish trousers," which became known as "bloomers," in her honor.[86] Fanny Kemble scandalized fellow visitors to the resort region of Lenox, Massachusetts, when she wore them, but idiosyncratic dress became an ongoing symbol of women's independence and autonomy.[87]

Indeed, this particular zone of conflict remained ongoing in the battle between the sexes, as it was not until the 1990s that women were allowed to wear pants on the U.S. Senate floor. Commentary on this topic has been such a part of the not-so-subtle gendered language that Hillary

Clinton's choice of pantsuits would be discussed as "wearing the pants" by members of the media during her time in the Senate.[88]

In the nineteenth century, too, stepping outside any gender boundaries could and did lead to sexualized and disparaging innuendo. During the Civil War, girls across the South faced unimaginable agonies, waiting for the death lists after any battle was announced. Some girls were so impatient to get out into the world that they confessed a longing to join the fight. Many younger women, particularly, believed that they might be able to serve their country, and find glory while in disguise. Lucy Breckenridge of Virginia bemoaned, "I wish that women could fight. I would gladly shoulder my pistol and shoot some Yankees if it were allowable. O, if I was only a man."[89] But if women dared to proverbially or literally wear the pants, then they would be subjected to verbal attacks or more. If women strayed from their proper sphere, they braved "public" exposure; and in the nineteenth century, "public women," meant they were women of the streets—indeed, the prostitutes and concubines of Massey's and others' dismissal.[90]

But "wearing the pants" might constitute something as innocent as expressing political opinion. Ladies were expected to remain reticent and proper, silent on matters men deemed their exclusive domain. This gendered clash of authority came to a head in the streets; indeed, the most infamous battle on this score erupted with Butler's occupation of New Orleans. Although Butler believed his Order No. 28 had tamed the wild women who plagued his troops in May 1862, he would be removed from his command shortly thereafter in December.

For a while, the women of the city seemed quiet, but defiance and Union displeasure came to a head in February 1863, when the federals gathered up as many Confederate prisoners as they could, to ship off for a prisoner exchange. Women responded in near-riotous fashion to the news of three hundred Confederate patriots gaining their freedom. The road to the waterfront became clogged with parasols and hoop skirts, and commanders attempted to dispel the women waving good-bye. It was a futile effort, and soon the entire waterfront was filled with women gaily waving handkerchiefs and refusing Gen. Nathaniel Banks any courtesy. Union commanders ordered naval officer Adm. David Farragut to stand ready to fire, but the ladies of New Orleans did not fear getting shelled—as they outnumbered and outmaneuvered. This incident was celebrated as "The Battle of the Handkerchiefs" to demonstrate the feeble way the Union command responded to the crisis. Waving handkerchiefs on the docks, smuggling military positions across enemy lines, braving jail cells to spy and disseminate critical intelligence—all these actions were part of Confederate women's defiance during wartime. Whether they were braving their new nation's restrictive gender dictates or the enemy's wrath, Rebel women could and did leave us traces of their bravado and their service.

Although we only have a fragmentary record for the less than two hundred women who ignored consequences to contemplate intelligence and military roles and to act on their impulses, these persistent females were nonetheless patriots. Neither the impermissibility of their cunning and courage nor the political incorrectness of their cause should disqualify them from our exploring their accomplishments. We may well disagree with their motives; we may hasten to point out their privileged and supremacist values. But even if we are rooting for them to fail at their counterrevolutionary campaigns, these spirited patriots require interrogation. Whatever their political and personal agendas, scholars might reframe and recast Confederate women's defiant careers in more balanced terms, in order to recognize women who seized the opportunity to serve their country—their country right or wrong.

# THREE

Mammy by Any Other Name

. . . that which we call a rose / By any other name would smell as sweet
—*ROMEO AND JULIET*

> and when we speak we are afraid
> our words will not be heard
> nor welcomed
> but when we are silent
> we are still afraid
> So it is better to speak
> remembering
> we were never meant to survive

—AUDRE LORDE, *LITANY FOR SURVIVAL*

Audre Lorde has suggested that "you cannot dismantle the master's house with the master's tools."[1] She is a powerful writer, a great thinker, as well as an inspiration to those who study her life and work. School-children who might read about her in my anthology, *I, Too, Sing America: Three Centuries of African American Poetry* (1998), will learn that she did not speak in school until the age of five. She later developed a voice to speak out with bravado, becoming a leading black woman intellectual at the end of the twentieth century. Another leading voice in this intellectual renaissance, bell hooks ("bell hooks" in lower case is her preferred usage), describes this impulse: "The longing to tell one's own story and the process of telling is symbolically a gesture of longing to recover the past in such a way that one experiences both a sense of reunion and a sense of release."[2]

In one of hooks's most stimulating books, *Talking Back: Thinking Feminist, Thinking Black,* she examines "naming" as a political act that remains "a serious process." And naming has been of crucial concern for many individuals within subordinated groups who struggle for self-recovery, for self-determination.[3] She goes on to remember that "in our southern black folk tradition we have the belief that a person never dies as long as their name is remembered, called. When the name bell hooks is called, the spirit of my great-grandmother rises." Thus, Gloria Watkins took on a new signature, recycled a name, but has not lost her identity; she has become bell hooks, the very model of a modern, self-invented persona. Hooks was not just about creating a name for herself or other African America women. She was struggling with the larger project of naming the nameless, dismantling without the master's tools.

Within the history of the Old South, "Mammy" presents modern historians, particularly scholars of southern women's history, with an un-pretty puzzle. "Mammy" is not a name but a stand-in for a name: a dystopic form of address which conjures up a body, while the person remains disembodied and anonymous.[4] Mammy as *brand* might be most apt. This term connotes a familiar and perhaps cherished type of manufactured product, while also invoking an identifying marker on burnt skin. This doubled imagery, at the cusp of the twenty-first century, evokes Mammy's propagandistic function above all. Most key to understanding this branding is recognizing that it's a white name for a black figure, a racial designation perpetrated by an oppressor.

The debate about Mammy continues today and might even be found within the corridors of power reshaping American capitalism. On August 5, 2015, the secretary of the Treasury and the U.S. treasurer invited a group of scholars to the Smithsonian to discuss ongoing efforts to put a female face on American currency.[5] This was part of several meetings around the country, and the U.S. Treasury launched its website soliciting advice on "The New Ten."[6] This Smithsonian summit elicited passionate opinions and heated exchanges. Scholars gathered from several fields—

from history and economics and anthropology—with specialists on time periods ranging from early America to late twentieth century, plus experts in numismatic studies, women's history, religious studies, indigenous peoples' studies, African American history, labor and immigration studies, and civil rights studies, among other topics.

Perhaps most surprising to me was one scholar's comment that the American people might not be prepared to accept a "Mammy" image on the money, even if it was the beloved icon, Harriet Tubman.

So there it was: Harriet Tubman—perhaps one of two black women in U.S. history with name recognition (the other being Rosa Parks)—defying invisibility by surviving, achieving, and escaping forces of erasure. She might be up against the Mammy, but she was also part of a new generation of African American scholarship that included "disremembering" alongside omitting. She would be part of a revised narrative that allowed flesh-and-blood women—as fleshy and bloody as necessary—to replace cartoon characters. That narrative included stories as fantastic as that of a little girl called Araminta, enslaved along Maryland's Eastern shore, who self-liberated and renamed herself as Harriet Tubman, her name now famous in juvenile fiction and history textbooks as a symbol of the Underground Railroad. In late twentieth-century America, her legacy extended to the battered women's movement when shelters and rescue networks adopted her name, recognizing her significance as a survivor.[7] Tubman's story may indeed be unique, but it is also emblematic of African American women's struggles in the nineteenth century and into the modern era. And despite her accomplishments and recognition of her role, Tubman was and is proof that "Mammy" remains a weapon leveled against all black women by a culture obsessed with sexism and racism.

Although Harriet Tubman remains much beloved by twenty-first-century schoolchildren, her name has been strangely absent from the annals of the academy. Until very recently, little was known of her accomplishments beyond folkloric associations with the Underground Railroad, and only in the twenty-first century have new studies highlighted her dynamic Civil War career. Only since April 20, 2016 when the U.S. Treasury made its announcement about putting Tubman on the currency (replacing Jackson on the $20 bill) has she become a household name.

Her first biography, a tribute volume written by her friend and patron Sarah Bradford in 1869, included a frontispiece that portrayed Tubman in her wartime garb, holding a rifle. This modest volume was not followed by another biographical study until 1943. During the second half of the twentieth century, the more than fifty books written about her were produced exclusively for children and young adults. In 2004, three new biographical studies of Tubman appeared—my own included; her reputation has been on the rise every since

Born into slavery in the third decade of the nineteenth century, Harriet Tubman lived well into the second decade of the twentieth. She emancipated herself by running away from her Maryland owner in 1849 and joined the growing cadre of black freedom fighters in the North. Committed to the battle against slavery, she took on the dangerous role of rescuing others, and conducted hundreds of fugitives to freedom along networks established by the Underground Railroad (UGRR). Not content to be a conductor—ferrying refugees from one safe house to the next— Tubman became what was known as an "abductor," an intrepid guide who would venture into slaveholding territory to shepherd escapees to safety and freedom—at first to the North and then across the border into Canada.

During the 1850s, she became a beloved figure among white and black abolitionists—revered as "Moses" within antislavery circles, at home and abroad. Her infamy grew among slaveholders, who railed against her bold abductions. I want to expand beyond her role in the UGRR, but this remarkable chapter of her life deserves all the attention it has garnered. During her own lifetime, her recollections of rescues held audiences, white and black, enthralled. For more than a century afterward, young Americans have been particularly inspired by Tubman's example as a person who dedicated herself to helping others, who let her light shine to lead the way for others. But all Americans would be better informed if they learned about her illustrious wartime career, when she was a freedom fighter behind enemy lines whose transformative work deserves more recognition than any association with a Mammy label.

Tubman actively worked on behalf of the Union, moving her "underground" struggle above ground. She first joined the Union military in

Virginia at Fortress Monroe, doing traditional female war work. But in 1862 she was drafted by Gov. John Andrew of Massachusetts to sail for occupied South Carolina with ninety other Yankee volunteers. When she landed at her strategic coastal outpost, Tubman assisted the hundreds, then thousands, of fugitives flowing through Beaufort into Union army camps.

Tubman served as a cook, nurse, and laundress for both civilians and soldiers. She was sent as far afield as Fernandina, Florida, on expeditions to assist federal troops. Then she used her skills to plan a raid up the Combahee River, one of the most daring Union operations in wartime Carolina. On June 2, 1863, shortly before midnight, three federal ships moved cautiously upriver, loaded with the soldiers of the Second South Carolina. The band of 150 black soldiers knew that on this mission their lives had been entrusted not just to their commander, Col. James Montgomery, but to the woman John Brown had called "General Tubman."

A sneak attack in the dead of night, to catch slaveholders off guard in their own backyards, was vintage Tubman. The plan resembled the times when she would return to Maryland under the nose of her former slaveholder and guide her brothers to freedom. By the summer of 1863, Union troops were restless. African American soldiers were untested by combat, but because of the hard fight to get them in the ranks, Union commanders in South Carolina were eager to push them to perform. Finally, they decided to risk sending men into the interior, even greenhorn colored troops, based on Tubman's assessment of enemy strength and positions. Along the Combahee, Tubman had scouted and found enslaved men and women willing to trade information for liberation, and that information insured the raid's ultimate success. She was able to pinpoint the location of Rebel torpedoes (stationery mines planted below the surface of the water) and guided federal ships to avoid them. This strategy enabled a tremendous surprise attack on the Carolina interior.

During this historic journey, she was liberating more than the handfuls at a time she had helped to freedom during her UGRR days; in one night, more than 750 enslaved South Carolinians were ferried to safety on Union boats. On the lookout, Tubman guided the pilots to designated spots along the shore where she had instructed fugitive slaves to hide.

Once given the all clear, they would approach the waterline to be loaded onto ships to cast their lots with "Mr. Lincoln's army."

The Union operation proceeded like clockwork. Near dawn, a Confederate described, "[Tubman] passed safely the point where the torpedoes were placed and finally reached the . . . ferry, which they immediately commenced cutting way, landed to all appearances a group at Mr. Middleton's and in a few minutes his buildings were in flames."[8] The horror of this attack on the celebrated Middleton Place drove the point home. This showplace estate represented slave power over the generations. Henry Middleton had served as governor of South Carolina, then ambassador to Russia from 1820 to 1830. The extended Middleton family owned several estates in the region and was one of the wealthiest clans in the state. Robbing warehouses and torching such planter homes was an added bonus for black soldiers, striking hard and deep at the proud master class.

Tubman's scheme was a resounding success. The official Confederate report concluded, "The enemy seems to have been well posted as to the character and capacity of our troops and their small chance of encountering opposition, and to have been well guided by persons thoroughly acquainted with the river and country."[9] Tubman described blacks as a fifth column, restless on low-country plantations, eager to anticipate the Union invasion. Many enslaved men wished to join the Union army but would do so only after federal troops transported their families to safety. Enlisted African Americans were satisfied to be able to throw scorn back at the enemy—and to prove to northern white comrades that "colored troops" were well worth their mettle.

After the Combahee River Raid, critics North and South could no longer pretend that enslaved people were unfit for battle; indeed their unique role was highlighted by this successful raid. This well-executed military operation using "colored troops" provided a bonus: aside from gaining a victory and humiliating the enemy, the enemy was reminded of the loss of property that could follow such a setback. Tubman's exploits were widely reported; as the Boston Commonwealth exclaimed, "Col. Montgomery and his gallant band of 800 black soldiers, under the guidance of a black woman, dashed in to the enemies' country . . .

destroying millions of dollars worth of commissary stores, cotton and lordly dwellings, and striking terror to the heart of rebeldom, brought off near 800 slaves and thousands of dollars worth of property."[10] The military men recognized Tubman's skills at spying and gathering intelligence as she served in South Carolina, even if such contributions went unrecorded and uncompensated.

Tubman became so physically drained by her efforts in South Carolina—she was stationed there for over two years—that she was given leave in the summer of 1864. It was during her convalescence in Boston in August 1864 that she had her first (and perhaps only) encounter with Sojourner Truth. They met up as comrades and recognized one another's key role in the effort to defeat the slave power. While Truth supported Abraham Lincoln and campaigned for his reelection in the fall of 1864, Tubman stuck to serving the soldiers.

Tubman's hypnagogic episodes (perhaps stemming from a youthful head injury), during which she would "lose time," became worse during wartime exertions. After her medical furlough, Tubman wanted to return to service in South Carolina, but she was having a hard time. While in Washington, D.C., awaiting military transport in the early months of 1865, she was drafted to assist federal forces in Virginia. She ended up, once again, at Fortress Monroe, where she took a position as a matron, caring for sick and wounded black soldiers. Within a month of her taking on her new post, Confederates surrendered, and Lincoln was assassinated.

During her return visit to Fortress Monroe, the bureaucracy and lack of supplies proved discouraging. So Tubman decided to leave Washington and return to the house she had purchased from Secretary of State William Seward, in Auburn, New York, which had served as the base of her UGRR operations since 1857. This residence offered her a sanctuary to which she might retreat and reunite with her parents and siblings, as well as a home community where she was supported. Tubman decided she would continue her reform activities in upstate New York by raising money for freedpeople's schools in the South.

Her homecoming was bittersweet, as on the journey back to the Fingerlakes region, she was denied her seat on a railcar. It took four men to eject her from it and haul her into the baggage car, where she was forced to remain until she debarked. Tubman was denied her rightful place and only ejected because white male authorities did not believe a black woman could merit a military pass.

Back in Auburn, Tubman continued to devote herself to benevolence and working against the prejudice and discrimination to which she and her emancipated countrymen and women were daily exposed. By the 1870s, Tubman was described in the Auburn papers as a philanthropist. For many years, she sheltered the needy and infirm in her own household, but in 1908 she was finally able to realize a dream and establish her charity, the "Harriet Tubman Home." In addition to this charity, she was outspoken on behalf of women's suffrage and other movements for social justice.

Her Civil War colleagues had supported her efforts to obtain a government pension for the work she had undertaken on behalf of the military. She was at first given a widow's pension in 1893, due to her marriage to former Union soldier, Nelson Davis. Private Davis had met Tubman when they were both serving in the occupied South. He relocated to Auburn, New York, following his discharge in Brownsville, Texas, and they married in 1869. Davis died of tuberculosis in 1888. Tubman received the modest death benefit allowed a soldier's wife but continued her campaign to have her *own* war service acknowledged. Congress finally recognized her singular contribution, but it took until 1899 for Tubman's personal pension to come through. She died in 1913, having fought hard and received the recognition she deserved as a heroic volunteer for the Union, as a scout and spy, and as a soldier and a patriot, not as an obsequious Mammy figure.

A handful of black southern women have given us their Civil War stories, and a cadre of contemporary scholars provide insightful interrogations, but this scholarship remains underrepresented in Civil War volumes.[11] There are, however, African American women protagonists remarkable for their exceptionalism, and two, on whom I have written, remain invaluable reminders of what work remains to be done. Both Harriet Tubman and Susie King Taylor were born enslaved in the South, and the war proved a cataclysmic experience for each of them. Their experiences might be instructive, as well as emblematic of black southern women in the Civil War.

Taylor is the only black southern woman to serve with Union troops and leave us a record.[12] Her *Reminiscences of My Life in Camp* remains an invaluable memoir, the voice of one exemplary African American woman's Civil War. Her insights into her experience in rural Georgia, in Savannah, on the Sea Islands, from slavery to freedom, provide a substantial portrait of the era. Furthermore, Taylor reflected on the legacy of this experience when she published her story in 1902.[13]

Taylor was born on a Georgia plantation in 1848, the first child of an enslaved mother named Baker. Her grandmother was born in 1820, the granddaughter of an African slave brought to Georgia during the 1730s. Taylor went to live with her grandmother in Savannah, escaping the plantation when she was just a young girl. During her years in Savannah, she had white playmates willing to teach her to read and write, even though offering instruction to a slave was against the law.

One of her tutors abandoned his pupil to enlist with the Savannah Volunteer Guards when the war broke out in 1861. Taylor vividly recalled the shelling of Fort Pulaski, which prompted a return to the countryside to be with her mother: "I remember what a roar and din the guns made. They jarred the earth for miles."[14] When federals captured the fort, Taylor was ferried behind Union lines, onto St. Simon's Island. Because she could read and write, white Union officers drafted her, at the age of fourteen, to teach freed slaves. She married a black soldier, a sergeant with the first South Carolina Volunteers, and subsequently served alongside her husband as a nurse and laundress for the troops. Taylor practiced other skills as well, confiding, "I learned to handle a musket very well while in the regiment, and could shoot straight and often hit the target."[15] When Clara Barton came to the Sea Islands, Taylor worked alongside her and remained with her own regiment through February 1865.

After the war, Taylor resettled in Savannah and opened a school. But when her husband died in 1866, she faced an uncertain and unsettling future, as she was left "soon to welcome a little stranger alone." Pregnant and widowed, she struggled to survive. By 1868, Taylor had to close her school, and in 1872 she left her child to live with her parents while she took a live-in job as a domestic for a wealthy Savannah family.

Unlike most women of her race and class, she did not spend the rest of her years in this role, slavery's legacy. Rather, Taylor secured a job in Boston, was able to leave domestic service when she remarried, and embarked on a career as a clubwoman and civic activist. In 1902, she published the remarkable chronicle of her life, showcasing her Civil War service, a narrative with poignant insight. Despite the great rarity of her account, Taylor made a dramatic point near the end of her memoir—encouraging readers to be aware of the many more who sacrificed for this new birth of freedom, both black and white, and most pointedly, *women* and men. Her clarion call sounds across the generations: "There are many people who do not know what some of the colored women did during the war. There were hundreds of them who assisted the Union soldiers by hiding them and helping them to escape. Many were punished for taking food to the prison stockades for the prisoners . . . Others assisted in various ways the Union army. These things should be kept in history before the people. There has never been a greater war in the United States than the one of 1861, where so many lives were lost,—*not men alone but noble women as well*" (emphasis added).[16]

African American women have been absent not only from historical accounts of the Civil War but from any appreciation of its legacy for black women and the incredible transformations wrought. Instead of seeking out the flesh-and-blood women who contributed to the rebirth of American freedom during this era and after, the myth of the Mammy was carefully cultivated. Mammy became a shield for slaveholders, used to deflect the violence perpetrated by slavery against an entire race. Mammy's fraudulence was designed by whites—for whites—against blacks, one of the many perks of white privilege. She was intended to dissipate the most brutal aspects of interracial liaisons, to disguise black women's victimization and trapped position within this ugly, raw system. She remained a clever ploy intended to divert investigators from evidence, shifting attention to sensational insinuations.

Mammy origins flourished and grew to wield considerable literary influence during the antebellum era. She became a prime element of the "positive good" propaganda, which proslavery advocates promoted to counter the increase of abolitionist influence during the postrevolutionary era.[17] She made irregular appearances as a featured player in regional literature, for example, in the *Southern Literary Messenger*. In 1836, in the "Diary of an Invalid," a New Yorker is introduced to the loyal and faithful caretaker, "Mammy Marget," whose South Carolina master proclaims, "She was the most devoted and faithful servant I ever knew. I loved and venerated her next to my mother."[18]

The bio-mythography persists in the metanarrative that Mammy was loyal to her charge, and the child who grew up would remain doggedly devoted to his/her faithful faux-maternal figure into adulthood. This preposterous fable has saturated American popular culture and become a major trope of the plantation epic. Indeed, the death of Mammy—with the mistress nursing her beloved former attendant—was a popular image. Confederate memoirs often included an illustration of such a deathbed scene. This recreated scene blossomed at the turn of the twentieth century and much later was featured in the television miniseries of *Scarlett*, the 1994 "sequel" to *Gone With the Wind*.[19]

By the late antebellum era, the Mammy figure had a spotlighted role in the contested terrain of American race relations. She became a central bone of contention for northern and southern authors dueling over images of black womanhood, particularly in fiction and memoir. One of the most influential novels of the nineteenth century, *Uncle Tom's Cabin*, first appeared in serial form over forty weeks in the abolitionist periodical *The National Era* and sold over 300,000 copies in the United States when the novel was published in 1852. The book went on to sell over a million copies in Great Britain.

In this most popular of nineteenth-century American novels, Harriet Beecher Stowe's Aunt Chloe, Uncle Tom's wife, is addressed by Eva as "Mammy": "A round, black, shining face is hers. Her whole plump countenance beams with satisfaction and contentment from under her well-starched checked turban."[20] She blossomed as a popular character in the North throughout the century. Beginning with postwar magazine literature, characters such as Maum Rina, featured in a short story in *Harper's Magazine* (1866), were depicted "with her glistening black face and spotted turban, and her queer shapeless figure waddling."[21]

This beaming countenance became a trademark symbol in soft-pedaling human bondage alongside the "shining face" of slavery apologism. Her dominance in the most popular novel in twentieth-century America, Margaret Mitchell's *Gone With the Wind* (1936), demonstrated Mammy's legendary reign as the human face of America's whitewash of slavery. Who could accuse slaveholders of *mistreating* enslaved bondswomen, when so many were depicted not only as smiling and devoted but as "waddling" and "round," testifying to their being well fed.

The myth of the Mammy has outgrown any historical understanding of the role black women might have played within plantation households, southern history, and questions of race and gender. Literary studies began the stampede of investigations, particularly Trudier Harris's *From Mammies to Militants: Domestics in Black American Literature* (1982).[22] Theoretical meditations blossomed in the 1980s and 1990s, and on into twenty-first-century academic discourse.[23] Historical work soon followed suit. K. Sue Jewell in *From Mammy to Miss America and Beyond: Cultural Images and the Shaping of U.S. Social Policy* (1993) reminds us that "although the image of the Mammy originated in the South during slavery, it has permeated every region of the United States."[24] A bubble of studies has followed Jewell's work on the significance of the Mammy.[25]

From thoughtful narratives on the United Daughters of the Confederacy's Mammy memorial to provocative charting of Aunt Jemima trading her bandana for pearl earrings, scholars are mining rich veins of historical ore.[26] These collective narratives cast Mammy as the inner core of a mountain of material producing/exporting/exploiting racism, and Foucault suggested we might dig deeper to excavate buried treasure.[27] Mammy as an instrument of racial hegemony provides a powerful undercurrent within such scholarship—demonstrating the potency of her presence.

We are confronted by Mammy's Cupboard, a rural roadhouse on Highway 61 near Natchez, Mississippi, or the vintage racist collectibles for sale in a Paris department store (Le Bon Marche). Antique shops and flea markets from the Texas borderlands to Maine include Mammy memorabilia. The shops along Royal Street in New Orleans, the souvenir stores in Charleston, and the seaside stalls on St. Simon's Island display such tchotchkes—not remnants, but reproductions (bells, salt and pepper shakes, and cookie jars, to name a few of the most popular items) stamped "Made in China." There is a virtual industry tilted toward white privilege's nostalgia, marketed at any price.

But markets may surprise us: I have never been as taken aback as I was in Galway, Ireland, attending an Irish studies conference in 2011, when I wandered into a souvenir shop and found myself surrounded by banners and gifts, all labeled "Mammy." On that day in March, I discovered that "Mammy" is the term used by country folk of the Emerald Isle to describe their mothers—the fourth Sunday of Lent is Mother's Day in the Republic of Ireland. Even with the explanation that it's a term applied nostalgically within Irish culture, I found myself disturbed seeing "Mammy" plastered everywhere.

I decided to probe this colloquial usage to see if the roots were in Ireland, considering that the Irish were captured by the Vikings and taken in shiploads to Iceland to be sold as slaves. Was this part of the link between the Irish and enslavement? I went on a quest and found lots of writing to suggest that early American usage of the term derived from Gaelic roots: *Mamai* (ma-moy). But when I queried early modern scholars— Gaelic language experts, English linguists, and, most significantly, Irish historians—muddle rather than clarity resulted. Even Nicholas Canny and Gearoid O'Tuathaigh, two of the most distinguished historians of the island, each an emeritus professor at the National University of Ireland in Galway, could not offer a definitive answer.

Studying word origins is a favorite pastime of mine.[28] The Insular Celtic languages (those derived from the British Isles and not the Continental Celtic languages, of which there are many) are divided into two groups: the Brythonic, which include Breton, Cornish, Welsh, and the extinct dialect of Cumbric, and—of greater interest to me—the Goidelic languages, which can be most easily split into three. The least spoken is Manx (on the Isle of Man), and the most spoken is Irish, by those in Ireland as well as those part of the Irish Diaspora.[29] In Northern Ireland, where I took a chair in 2006 and lived full time for eight years, Irish and Ulster Scots languages regularly square off.[30]

Back to the subject at hand, I could find no authoritative agreement on the linguistic origins of *Mammy*—especially its American provenance. The *Oxford English Dictionary* credits the term to Anglo rather than Gaelic derivation. This is startling, with wider implications. Such "origins" discoveries, it would seem, are not uncommon. For example, Tyler Parry's University of South Carolina dissertation, "'Jis Lak . . . de White Folks': 'Jumping the Broom' as a Case Study in Exploring the Intercultural and Atlantic Dimensions of Southern Society" examines the Works Progress Administration (WPA) narratives and nineteenth-century sources. He found "jumpin' de broom" conspicuously absent from both contemporary records of nineteenth-century America and oral historical sources from the era and later periods. This suggests that the term might have more established roots within Great Britain than in Africa, despite the hype of American pop culture.

Certainly, "jumping the broom" can be recast with historical accuracy as part of the modern memory industry in the wake of the popularity of Kwanzaa—a celebration created by a black American scholar in 1966.[31] But whether jumping the broom was originated by Romany travelers in Wales or the Welsh themselves, or popularized by those who left the British Isles and transplanted customs to Appalachia, it has nevertheless been adapted by modern African American culture and entrenched within the popular imagination as a signifier.[32]

An urban dictionary confides that the term *Mammy* is rarely used but, if applied, can be considered an "ethnic slur." In Ireland and the UK, Mammy is still *widely* used as a synonym for mother by young people, without any racial connotation.[33] Yet the term has a class component, especially when contrasted with British usage of *mummy*. There is also a regional slant, as *mam* or *mammy* is more common in the North of England than in the South.

Whatever the linguistic origins of this term, it is a name with instant recognition. It is also the name of an American show tune popular throughout the twentieth century. "Mammy" was associated with the stage and film star Al Jolson, who sang it on Broadway in 1918 and popularized the tune in 1927 by singing it during the first "talkie," *The Jazz Singer*. This film was an international sensation, marking a dramatic leap forward from the silent era. Jolson sang "Mammy" in two subsequent feature films, and the song became one of his signature performances.[34] As Richard Corliss suggested in *Time*, Jolson would "build a tune to operatic grandeur, then tear it apart with a sobbing coda."[35] He performed in blackface, a practice embedded in the culture of the time, when mass entertainments featured white singers with burnt cork on their faces, performing from vaudeville stages to campgrounds all across America for nearly half a century.

The lyrics demonstrate the sentimentality showcased in the racialism associated with the Mammy figure:

> Everything seems lovely
> When you start to roam.
> The birds are singing the day that you stray.
> Everything seems lovely
> When you start to roam.
> The birds are singing the day that you stray.
> But wait until you are further away.
> Things won't be so lovely
> When you're all alone.
> Here's what you'll keep saying
> When you're far from home.
>
> Mammy, mammy,
> The sun shines east,
> The sun shines west,
> But I know where the sun shines best.
> Mammy, my little mammy,
> My heartstrings are tangled around Alabamy.
> I'm a'comin,
> Sorry that I made you wait.
> I'm a'comin,
> Hope and trust that I'm not late.
> Oh mammy, my little mammy,
> I'd walk a million miles for one of your smiles,
> My mammy.

"Mammy" remained a popular tune and was recorded frequently, even following the modern civil rights movement. Between the 1960s and into the 1990s, for example, the Everly Brothers, Liza Minelli, Cher, and Mandy Patinkin all included the song in concerts and released covers of the song. From jukebox to pancake box, Mammy bounded along in the cultural ether, even as millions of African American women struggled against this racist stereotype.

This struggle paid off; by the 1980s, the label—routinely slapped on thousands of anonymous women—faded from fashion. Mammy's iconic status deflated, as African American women writers, actors, activists, and artists replaced white projections with significant substitutes, flesh-and-blood nineteenth-century women such as the aforementioned Harriet Tubman, as well as Frances Harper Watkins, Hallie Brown, Sojourner Truth, Harriet Jacobs, Elizabeth Keckley, Anna Julia Cooper, Mary Mc-Cloud Bethune, and Alice Dunbar Nelson, to name just a few.

Within current historical discourse, Mammy is routinely sliced and diced—while her symbolism is interrogated by scores of critical theorists. Mammy does not pack the visceral punch of the term *nigger*, explored so imaginatively by Randall Kennedy in his book subtitled, "The Strange Career of a Troublesome Word."[36] I would suggest that the term *Uncle Tom* has been lobbed with more ferocity and frequency than *Mammy*, particularly in the 1960s. Accusing someone of being a "Tom" might have gone out of fashion, but the dissing term *Oreo*, indicating someone black "on the outside" and white "on the inside," remains a vitriolic charge.[37] At the same time, Mammy's demeanor in popular historical depictions is condemned as inauthentic, and even if a masque, this charade—despite any subversive possibilities—has overstayed its shelf life.

The debates spill into the twenty-first-century petition campaign to remove the image of Aunt Jemima from Quaker Oats Company products, as a critic railed: "Enough of the cruel barbs of Aunt Jemima's grinning, slavish, servile face that is a throwback to a time when black women were looked upon as only fit to serve the bottomless pit of others needs, all the while expected to deny their needs and right to respect. No more to Aunt Jemima. Enough is enough."[38] In the twenty-first century, Mammy is rarely employed as slander—rather she is more antiquarian than acidic.[39] "Sambo," "Uncle Ben," and "Uncle Tom" alongside "Aunt Jemima" and "Mammy" conjure up hurtful caricatures. These images have allegedly been banished to a "bygone era" (perhaps akin to claims that Barack Obama's election heralded a postracial era?).

Even if the term *Mammy* is applied as an anachronistic label, it has taken on a timelessness that belies historical contextualization. We associate the term *Mammy* with a vanished typology, but more truthfully, it is a trompe l'oeil that remains captured within the white mind's eye. How do nineteenth-century magazine renditions of this maternal figure stack up against Carson McCullers's compelling Bernice Brown in *A Member of the Wedding* (1946)?

The Mammy myth has outgrown any real or fictive appreciation of the role black women might have played within plantation households or slaveholders' memoirs. Too often, Mammies decorate the prose of white southern women's narratives (as described in Chapter 1). And they continued to serve as emblems in nineteenth-century American literature, intended as props to hold up crumbling racist regimes (with the notable exceptions of work by writers like Charles Chesnutt, Paul Laurence Dunbar, and Francis Ellen Watkins Harper). The flesh-and-blood women, rather than the superficial functionaries, remain, in a sense, in "another part of the forest." Lillian Hellman was praised in 1939 when "The Little Foxes," a Broadway play set in the post–Civil War South did not succumb to stereotypes in its treatment of black women, but she was an exceptional figure among white southern women authors in the twentieth century.[40]

Mammy is no longer a regional figure because, as K. Sue Jewell reminds us, "although the image of the Mammy originated in the South during slavery, it has permeated every region of the United States."[41] The promotional literature spreading her fame may have had Dixie origins, but a Yankee audience consumed and parroted this racist sentimentalism. Horace Greeley, a vocal antislavery author and statesman, wrote about white southern males: "the negro nature he especially knows, profoundly, intimately, knows it; not through the cold light of ethnographical science only, but most of all through the warm, enkindling recollections of boyhood and youth."[42]

A steady stream of monographs deconstructing her image and popularity has followed Jewell's pioneering work on Mammy's cultural persistence.[43] Again, much can be learned from exploring this new literature, including Micki McElya's *Clinging to Mammy: The Faithful Slave in Twentieth-Century America* (2007) and Kimberly Wallace-Sanders's *Mammy: A Century of Race, Gender, and Southern Memory* (2008).[44]

Individually, each author gives us a raft of brilliant insights; cultural readings and analytical breakthroughs abound.[45] We gain an appreciation of Mammy as a figure trotted out to telegraph a complex set of codes—a cultural product disguised as historical personage. Quite naturally, this campaign of dissemblance focused on the plantation household—a battleground. I have written elsewhere on the explosive nature of sex, race, and intimacy within this nexus—the Mammy is meant to neutralize indictments of slaveholders, particularly the predatory nature of this system. "My family black and white" was a phrase offered up by antebellum southern patriarchs without a hint of irony. In the twentieth century, there was concerted resistance on the part of scholars of the Old South to recognize sexual predatory practices as a part of slavery; rather, many clung to romanticized notions, including Eugene Genovese, who proclaimed in *Roll, Jordan, Roll:* "But most men, even most free-wheeling, gambling, whoring young aristocrats, do not readily indulge their sadistic impulses. It would be hard to live with a submissive young woman for long and to continue to consider her mere property or a mere object of sexual gratification, especially since the free gift of her beauty has so much more to offer than her yielding to force."[46] This passage is framed by a discussion of *Twelve Years a Slave* and afterward a suggestion that many enslaved concubines, like their "free quadroon sisters in New Orleans," may have ended up falling in love with men who forced them to have sex. This suggestion elicited an extended critique in my first book, *The Plantation Mistress,* and continues to stir up objections.[47]

Annette Gordon-Reed edited a book in my series Viewpoints of American Culture (Oxford University Press) a few years before winning the Pulitzer Prize for her study of the Hemings family. At the time, I was working on a book chapter on interracial liaisons between white men and black women from Thomas Jefferson to Strom Thurmond, from Sally Hemings to Essie Mae Washington-Williams.[48] I wanted to label the males within these "couples" as "sexual predators," but Gordon-Reed insisted that I shift my focus to look at "sexual hypocrisy"—to forego the topic of "predators."[49] Historians continue to have complicated perspectives on victimization and agency, particularly for the study of African American women and more particularly of enslaved women in the Americas.[50]

Revisionist work on African Americans during the Civil War and Reconstruction has encouraged us to look at black women as historical actors rather than as the mythical symbols of black womanhood whites have projected. An eagerly anticipated manuscript, Thavolia Glymph's *Out of the House of Bondage: The Transformation of the Plantation Household* (2008), fulfilled scholars' high expectations.[51] She persuasively demonstrated how the plantation household was a political space where enslaved women and white women battled over labor, kin, and autonomy. She also interrogated the bloody clashes over freedom and citizenship during the period immediately following the Civil War.

Glymph's study built on the suggestion by Elizabeth Fox-Genovese that plantation mistresses represented "the feminine face of paternalism." Glymph's work provides a bounty of evidence and analytical gravitas to undermine prevailing notions that the private world of the plantation household was not as treacherous a terrain as the agricultural fields. She persuasively suggests that violence and politics were far from removed from the private sphere; rather, the cauldron of contradictions often boiled over, with explosive results. Glymph asserts that the major culprits directing violent acts toward black women were plantation mistresses, who could and did execute power against enslaved women.[52]

By closely interrogating interactions between enslaved and slaveholding women during the antebellum period, Glymph does not recognize the Civil War as a watershed moment in which white women gained an unprecedented degree of authority and became more involved in plantation management.[53] Instead, she argues that in the decades leading up to the war, most white slaveholding women were actively involved in their bondspeople's lives, so much so that they could and did violently coerce many into performing backbreaking labor and exact punishment for insubordination. Drew Faust's notion that women only gained mastery with wartime experiences does not fit neatly with Glymph's structural analysis.

These clashes between Glymph's and Faust's theses might be reconciled, as any field of American history defies unified interpretation. In the many plantation households strewn across the southern landscape, it is likely that the Civil War did, in fact, mobilize slaveholding women as Faust argues, but surely many had already demonstrated their distinctive talents at mastery long before the firing on Fort Sumter, as Glymph maintains. Debates continue over women's roles on wartime plantations, and with over 4 million bondspeople held on farms and estates across the Confederate South from rural Maryland to the Texan frontier, complexities and variations create competing scenarios.

Glymph offers evidence of white women's authority and participation in the maintenance of the slavocracy. In making the claim that slaveholding women possessed the power to execute violent acts, Glymph, in a dazzling analytic turn, makes significant contribution to historical interpretations of elite southern white women. While much of the scholarship is focused on mistresses' resistance to societal norms and their struggles for empowerment, Glymph contrarily presents white women seeking status and power by abusing those over whom they maintained sway, particularly black women.[54]

White mistresses, Glymph suggested, relied on both the image and the presence of enslaved women in their households in order to appear more "civilized." She reveals how all of this changed dramatically after the Civil War when African American women made strides toward authority, while white women felt the ground below them shifting. Glymph emphatically proposes that the war did not significantly alter relations between black and white women on plantations: relationships remained ruled by class and race, and the typology remained coercive violence. Her framework and steadfast absolutism has become the leading interpretation of the period. Rather than piling up evidence and counterclaims, scholars such as myself suggest more nuanced interpretations, informed by Glymph's powerful insights. At the same time that I accept her perspective on this era, I remain skeptical that these relations remained so tethered to violence.

If claims are made that white women were enforcers on plantations, following up on Fox-Genovese's arguments that women were power hungry and sought autonomy through authority, then aspects of Stanley Elkins's controversial work, *Slavery: A Problem in American Institutional and Intellectual Life* (1959) might offer glimmers of illumination. Were plantation mistresses the prison guards, unquestioningly following orders, with masters as dictatorial and brutal wardens, ruling from on high? What was the relationship between guards and prisoners, and how did race, gender, and sex interact within this plantation as prison, a dystopian Foucauldian formula?

Antebellum estates, particularly in the deep South, have only recently been revisited as the crossroads of violence and oppression. In December 2014, the Whitney Plantation Museum outside New Orleans, Louisiana, used heads on poles as an opening gambit. (They have since been removed.) The year before, we were shown the monstrous estate to which Solomon Northup was exiled in Steve McQueen's much-heralded film *Twelve Years a Slave* (2013). We are in the midst of a much-needed renaissance of powerful and creative work dictating new terms of analysis—including Stephen Small's forthcoming study of heritage tourism on plantations, as well as artist Kara Walker's string of acidic portraits of plantation life. This significant project of awakening the American public, particularly white Americans, to U.S. slavery's dehumanizing aspects—and its legacy—has been an ongoing intervention. Glymph's clarion call is being heeded on several levels, with her influence acknowledged most recently in the award-winning work of Ta-Nehisi Coates, *Between the World and Me*.[55]

Glymph's careful research incorporates voices of African Americans, the lost testimonies of black eyewitnesses who stand sentinel against the legions of sentimental racialists who allowed Mammy to stand in for the flesh-and-blood women who endured the death throes of slavery during the Civil War. Again, new scholarly studies are highlighting the personal alongside the political, deconstructing transitions wrought by those enslaved as they struggled to liberate themselves and their loved ones.

Spottswood Rice was able to rescue his wife and five of his seven children from his former owner, Kitty Diggs. He wrote to his girls left behind in bondage from a military hospital near St. Louis in 1864: "my respects is worn out and have no sympathy for Slaveholders. And as for her cristianantty [the mistress's] I expect the Devil has such in hell. You tell her from me that she is the frist Christian that I ever hard say that aman could Steal his own child especially out of human bondage." His bravado stemmed perhaps from the fact that even as he lay in a hospital bed, he planned their rescue: "8 hundred White and 8 hundred blacke solders expects to start up the rivore to Glasgow . . . when they Come I expect to be with, them and expect to get you both in return. Dont be uneasy my children."[56]

Desperate circumstances caused drastic results. One Kentucky woman spirited her children away, only to be accosted by her master's son-in-law, "who told me that if I did not go back with him he would shoot me. He drew a pistol on me as he made this threat. I could offer no resistance as he constantly kept the pistol pointed at me."[57] She was forced to return home at gunpoint, while the white man kidnapped her seven year old as hostage.

Eliza Scantling, fifteen in 1865, remembered how she "plowed a mule an' a wild un at dat. Sometimes me hands get so cold I jes' cry."[58] For enslaved children, the prospect of an invading enemy was confusing and, at times, terrifying. Mittie Freeman, at ten, hid in a tree when the first bluecoats arrived. As slave men fled the plantations, many left women and children behind. During wartime, thousands were fatherless and many hundreds orphaned. Women and children have been given a cameo role in this history, but scholars of the period are now beginning to take seriously the significance of these transitions.

In the transition from slavery to freedom, the integrity of the black woman's body became a hotly contested terrain.[59] Whites raised the shibboleth of the moral inferiority of black women, and African American spokeswomen, from the Civil War onward, fought back. By the end of the century, the politics of respectability entered into the discourse, and battle lines were being drawn. Fannie Barrier Williams, active in Chicago black reform groups, politicked within the women's organization in charge of the Chicago Columbian Exposition of 1893. When black women's participation met with opposition, Williams spoke out: "I regret the necessity of speaking to the question of the moral progress of our women, because the morality of our home life has been commented on so disparagingly and meanly that we are placed in the unfortunate position of being defenders of our name."[60] Williams was able to take on an official role in charge of "Colored Interests in the Department of Publicity and

Promotions" for the exposition. She offered lectures and participated in forums with Anna Julia Cooper and Fannie Jackson Coppin, as well as Frederick Douglass.

Anna Julia Cooper was a Washington educator and leading black intellectual. In 1892, she published *A Voice From the South,* one of the first major texts of black feminism. Cooper's role as principal of the preeminent M Street High School in Washington, D.C. (renamed the Dunbar School after the death of writer Paul Dunbar in 1906), put her in contact with African American leaders from around the country. She was invited to address the World Congress of Women, which met in Chicago in 1893.

Clearly, during the turn of the century, the public denigration of African American women led black women to champion female purity and to deny the demeaning stereotype of black females as women of "easy virtue." A black spokeswoman, Josephine St. Pierre Ruffin of Boston, denounced racially segregated federations and attacked white women's hypocrisy: "Year after year southern women have protested against the admission of colored women into any national organization on the grounds of immorality of these women . . . The charge has never been crushed, as it could and should have been at first."[61] Black women knew that, in many instances, it was the predatory practices of white women's husbands, brothers, and sons (not to mention fathers) that created sorrowful patterns of dangerous "liaisons." The rare white southern woman in the early twentieth century might have been willing to confront these explosive topics, but it was only black women who tackled this tangle of issues in the post–Civil War South.

Lily Hardy Hammond was a prolific writer who has been relatively neglected by scholars working on race. But due to a new collection of her writings, *In Black and White: An Interpretation of the South,* edited by Elna Green, we can explore more readily Hammond's radical vision.[62] Like Angelina Grimké nearly a hundred years before, Hammond directly addressed her white southern sisters on the burning issues of the day: "You say, in effect, that morality in a Negro doesn't count. You teach your sons that from babyhood. The Negro women pay for it; but by God's law your sons pay, too—pay a debt more yours than theirs. And the daughters they pay too."[63]

Calling out white men—or, even more outrageously, confronting white women raising sons—on this issue of predatory conduct was a radical measure. Frank discussion was deadly during a time when white racists continued to suggest that lynching was the only way to handle the problem of white women's protection from the "black beast rapist." [64] During the 1890s, corpses dangling from nooses dotted the southern landscape—with a lynching every other day throughout much of the decade, mainly in southern states. (Nearly 25% of those murdered were white, perhaps those willing to make sympathetic claims or in any way interfere with the absolute power of "Judge Lynch" in the region.)

This complicated period of slavery's legacy, coupled with more sophisticated interrogation of interracial sex, has stimulated engaging scholarly debate. And, as Annette Gordon-Reed pointed out in 2009:

> There's also a lot of white Southern anxiety in denials of these tangled blood lines. Acknowledging them requires admitting what went on in the South; both the prevalence of the rape of black women and, in some instances, long-term connections between white men and black women in slavery and outside of it. The evidence indicates that Southern white men of the 18th and 19th centuries were more used to sleeping with black women than white men today in all regions of the country; despite the popular notion that we're living in a brand new age of interracial mixing. Some of those planters really were living like polygamous patriarchs of old with wives and concubines and bunches of kids. That's the truth of early American history. [65]

Over twenty years ago, I meditated on this matter in "'With a Whip in His Hand': Rape, Memory, and African-American Women," an essay published in a volume emerging from a working group at the W. E. B. Du Bois Center at Harvard University, an international, interdisciplinary group headed by Geneviève Fabre and the late Melvin Dixon. This volume, *History and Memory in African-American Culture,* explored literature, fiction, film, and dance and included essays by David Blight and Nellie McKay, among others. [66] It was one of the first American volumes to examine *les lieux de memoires* (a phrase that launched countless memory studies), and it included an essay by Pierre Nora. It was also a volume in which African American women's intersecting issues of gender, race, sexuality, and violence were given serious historical consideration within an interdisciplinary format. This field has been blossoming dramatically, and exciting new scholarship is showcased in a forthcoming anthology, *Sexuality and Slavery: Creating an Intimate History of the Americas*, edited by Daina Ramey Berry and Leslie Harris.

One of the most outspoken writers, thinkers, and activists on issues of gender and race, violence and sexuality was Ida B. Wells-Barnett, who, born enslaved in Mississippi, became a leading journalist and activist spokeswoman headquartered in Chicago. After the lynching of close friends, Wells printed the truth about the murders. Her press was smashed, and she was threatened with bodily harm. She fled to Chicago to continue her anti-lynching campaign, where she married the editor and lecturer Ferdinand Barnett and became one of the first prominent black women activists to hyphenate her last name, becoming known as Ida B. Wells-Barnett. Despite her children—the couple eventually had four offspring—Wells-Barnett struggled to maintain her rigorous travel and speaking schedule, becoming an internationally known crusader for African American rights.

Black leaders fumed at the tokenism of white organizers declaring August 25, 1893, as Colored American Day at the Chicago World's Fair. Having experienced firsthand the rampant prejudice among organizers of the Columbian Exposition, Wells-Barnett prepared a booklet for distribution: "The Reason Why the Colored American is not in the World's Columbian Exposition." She would launch an international crusade against lynching and continue to agitate within and outside the United States for an end to racism's most brutal by-product, the mob execution of hundreds of men and women every year, mainly in the South.[67]

The demolition of racist stereotypes continued to be an active campaign, particularly for black clubwomen. Mary Church Terrell (along with Wells-Barnett) was a founder of the National Association of Colored Women's Clubs and built a movement dedicated to uplift and desegregation. Authors Charles Chesnutt and Pauline Hopkins were two of the many black writers at the turn of the century whose work dealt powerfully with American racism and contributed to an alternate universe for American literature.

Within this universe, readers might explore issues of moral culpability, darkness, and light in ways that had been largely ignored within white America. But again, southern African American women, especially those who migrated North, found themselves rocked back on their heels by the brute force of racism and sexism.

While Anna Julia Cooper was addressing a women's congress on the progress of black women, the only black women within the "White City," as the midway of the Columbian Exposition was called, were servants or women put on exhibition as "darkies." (Paul Laurence Dunbar worked at the fair as a lavatory attendant, and James Weldon Johnson held an equally menial post.) One featured African American, Nancy Green, had been hired to dress in costume and flip pancakes to promote a new business venture: a pancake mix company, founded by Charles Rutt, with the trademark "Aunt Jemima." Rutt manufactured a foundational story on which he could build his pancake empire: a Confederate general returned to the South to seek out the woman who had made him pancakes during the war, and he convinced her to sell him her recipe. Rutt decided to debut his "living trademark" in 1893 at the World's Fair, where Green and her pancakes were a "hit"—along with the fictionalized narrative of the company.[68]

The company soon introduced Aunt Jemima paper dolls and, ten years later, rag dolls. Aunt Jemima's beaming face became a symbol not just of pancakes but of an entire range of racial etiquette and coda, which several scholars have deftly tackled, including Maurice Manring in *Slave in a Box: The Strange Career of Aunt Jemima*.[69] Like Mammy, Aunt Jemima is not intended to represent a single woman but rather the black everywoman of white fantasy, a woman who enjoyed her subservience and dedicated herself to the service of others. She had no life of her own but remained the floating figure of comfort. As K. Sue Jewell argues, "two of Mammy's most endowed features are her breasts and her buttocks . . . the unusually large buttocks and embellished breasts place mammy outside the sphere of sexual desirability and into the realm of maternal nurturance . . . [This] allows the males who constructed this image, and those who accept it, to disavow their sexual interests in African American women." Indeed, modern incarnations of Mammy are carefully cultivated falsehoods, as when film producers stipulated in contracts that Louise Beavers, who frequently played a Mammy character in films, must keep her weight at two hundred pounds to maintain her screen image.[70]

The caricatures of black women as mere Mammies are not just a troubling aspect of American cultural history and an ugly legacy of slavery; they have serious impact on Civil War studies. The scholarship on the American Civil War—one of the largest subfields within U.S. history—promotes the funding of research centers; publication in prestigious journals across the country; the annual organization of academic conferences, workshops, and public history programs; the granting of PhDs and hiring of new faculty; the establishment of name chairs; and several prestigious book prizes. Unlike so many other historical epochs, this war of four years has produced a mountain of scholarly and popular literature and continues its tenacious hold on American audiences, with weekly programs broadcast on C-Span and annual events at Gettysburg College and at the Abraham Lincoln Presidential Library in Springfield, Illinois. Representations of black women very much matter within this burgeoning field.

As historian Jim Downs notes, black people are often projected as robust political actors during the Civil War—perhaps in response to specific schools of thought which have hitherto attempted to separate the issue of slavery and the prolonged siege of war from 1861 to 1865.[71] It is also part of a vibrant political agenda that seeks to counter present-day racism, portraying black people in freedom as disengaged from patriotism and politics. Historiographically, renewed and vigorous appreciations of black activism began to proliferate in the 1970s, as Downs argues, and shattered the prevailing racist themes embraced by the Dunning school. Those Reconstruction scholars who followed in the footsteps of William Dunning of Columbia University preached a fairly rigid party line—that Black Reconstruction was a failure—and this school of historians blamed the victims more than those in power.[72] As Eric Foner has suggested, historical interpretations could create powerful and practical applications: "The traditional or Dunning School of Reconstruction was not just an interpretation of history. It was part of the edifice of the Jim Crow System."[73] By dismantling a school of thought, you can pull the rug out from under those who use historical arguments to justify continuing oppression.

A new generation of scholars—nerved by civil rights protest—powerfully demonstrates the possibilities of social change linked to compelling and radical archival research. They continue to uncover repositories, locate sources, and develop creative ways to find black people in the records, even those collected by white institutions, many with racist agendas. Accidents happen when what is preserved is seen by new sets of eyes. As Downs suggests, the bulk of the Freedmen's Bureau records in many ways painted the broad brushstrokes of concern that post–civil rights historians harbored toward freedpeople in the 1970s. Many scholars handling these materials follow a rote rhetorical pattern, portraying emancipated slaves as indefatigable heroes. In other words, they replaced a caricature with an emblem (one stereotype with another?)—thus addressing the historical record with targeted correctives. It is a defensive position, which demands a weighted response. Fortunately, we may now incorporate some of the insights shared by African American women themselves, such as Frances Harper, who complained when black men beat their wives and warned that "their subjection has not ceased in freedom."[74]

Harper's warning has been lost on a generation of historians who are determined to present black people as heroes of their age and who, fearing the taint of stereotype, may be unwilling to reveal the full human dimensions of African Americans of this era. Interrogating other records that highlight black life in the past—for example, the WPA records—creates a vibrant debate among historians about merits and drawbacks. A similar discourse about the Freedmen's Bureau documents, Downs explains, has not yet fully developed; instead, most often, these records are uncritically heralded, based on the laudable efforts of the historians who have found and organized them.

However, raising the issue that enslaved and freedpeople may not have had agency or did not effectively demonstrate political action does not support white supremacy or black subordination. If anything, such a claim does exactly the opposite and reveals the full complexity and uniqueness of the situation of newly "freed" people and their humanity. Most likely, Audre Lorde would scold us for using the very language of emancipation, which betrays our enchantment with the master's tools.

Noralee Frankel has suggested that the roots of this stall-out began in the wake of the war: "The inability of former slaveholders to comprehend freedom's appeal or accept the reality of emancipation helped poison race relations after the war."[75] Certainly, Freedmen's Bureau agents might slip comfortably into patterns of discrimination themselves. As they portrayed black women so unfavorably, they helped poison the well. In the summer of 1866, J. D. Harris of the Georgia Bureau complained, "They are found occupying all the vacant houses in the villages and country that they can get into, loitering and lounging about, some of them pretending an occupation but most of them sponging upon the scanty earnings of their Fathers Husbands and friends."[76] The racism ricochets right off the page, as Harris, a white soldier from the North, excoriates black women for their dependency—on black men! Telling these stories remains challenging, with such observations as Harris's often telling us so much more about the distortions within the white mind than about the lives of the African Americans described.

Political agendas still collide with political correctness in scholarship, but emblematic individuals often lose their flatness and can sizzle and sting in the hands of novelists. Therefore, many great black women writers—from Zora Neale Hurston to Lorraine Hansberry to Toni Morrison—reveal African American protagonists who make mistakes, take the "wrong path," and are no candidates for sainthood.[77] Representativeness may be lost in the charisma of character, with a nod toward familiar truths. Invisibility, which has long plagued African American women, has only recently been addressed within the academy and publishing world, with mixed results.[78]

In her 1987 essay, "The Darkest Eye," Mary Helen Washington argued: "If there is a single distinguishing feature of the literature of black women—and this accounts for their lack of recognition—it is this: their literature is about black women; it takes the trouble to record the thoughts, words, feelings, and deeds of black women, experiences that make the realities of being black in America look very different from what men have written."[79] It is no surprise that when black women began to assert their own voices, a backlash developed early on—pitted against black men in a racist and sexist marketplace, they were not just under siege from the white literati.[80]

Taking the trouble to record thoughts, words, feelings, and deeds of black women has been a struggle within southern women's history and African American history as well—why move beyond when the Mammy has sufficed? Developing new ways of thinking about African American women's historical experience and connecting these to contemporary audiences make this a rich and emerging field. Certainly, Thavolia Glymph's occasional invocation of first person, combined with the elegant tone and style of her personal delivery, makes valuable inroads. Saidiya Hartman's *Lose Your Mother*—a book that placed Hartman at the core of analysis of the Atlantic slave trade—creates equally powerful vibrations in the field. This new crossover perspective in some way inverts the Lost Cause literature of a century ago and creates a funhouse mirror of revisionist reflection.[81]

Glymph justifies the meditative qualities of her project by calling hers a work-in-process; yet, scholars should not shy away from this approach in larger projects. Using meditation as a framework enables Glymph to discuss nuance and raise questions that too often remain unspoken. Her example allows the historian to enter the story and, most of all, permits her to introduce fragmentary evidence where most historians build their projects around as complete a set of data as possible. What if scholars begin to put the "personal is political" into practice within the academy—not just burying these concerns in the scholarly apparatus but placing them front and center.[82] Further, as Downs has powerfully argued, what if the organizing principle of a book project lay in a commitment to a fragmentary and fractured body of evidence? What if the scraps of evidence dictated the argument and the arc? Some historians—Tera Hunter and Jennifer Morgan, for example—have done this, and their accomplishments argue for more scholars to take this on.[83]

While most researchers operate from the premise that only the fully complete archival dataset can properly limn a period, things are changing. What if the glimpses provided by the incomplete archive offer a more authentic view than the relentless hoard of what was preserved for posterity? The preserved records about black people during the Civil War and Reconstruction, as in the case of the Freedmen's Bureau records, survived for a reason. These documents reflect the bureaucratic and administrative functions of the official story and the ideological positions of a cohort of federal officials as much as they show "what happened." What if these scraps of evidence can give us new inroads into the mountain of material available for the Civil War—blasting with dynamite to get a hole through it? Why climb over when you can just tunnel through?

I did my undergraduate work at Harvard nearly fifty years ago, earning my degree in the early 1970s in what was called the Department of Afro-American Studies, when only scraps of evidence were being assembled. At this time, aligning with Afro-American Studies was a political act. This particular department had been born out of protest, and it survived only because of renewed student activism in the 1980s.[84]

These 1980s campus protests were powerful reminders, which energized me to join the Department of African American Studies as a visiting lecturer—if only temporarily—between the death of a wonderful man and mentor, Nathan Huggins, and the department's resurrection into the leading intellectual center it has become for African American Studies, nationally and globally. The department was kept on life support—thanks to very committed stewards such as Werner Sollors and the late Barbara Johnson—until a permanent leader, Henry Louis Gates Jr., took up the reins in 1991 and transformed the department and the W. E. B. DuBois Research Institute into a juggernaut.

Theoretical work remains *vital* to the field, but I always end up being a resistant audience member, listening as the linguist explains patiently about the use of negative and positive terms, and reminds that a negative *can* be a positive, and a positive *can* be a negative and a double negative *can* be positive but a double positive can *never* be a negative. Then someone from the back derisively chimes in: "Yeah, yeah."

The battle over interpreting freedwomen began long ago and has not yet gained *enough* traction. This project must involve as much elbow grease (to borrow an obsolete phrase) as poststructuralism: too much is at stake to leave this field to pockets of academics snarking over abstractions. While we wrestle with theoretical nuance and academic imprecision, the histories of black southern women during the Civil War and Reconstruction are "obscured and uncelebrated." When I wrote this phrase nearly a quarter century ago, I was standing on a relatively empty, if not barren, ground. We did not yet have the multivolume *Freedom: A Documentary History of Emancipation 1861–67* (1985–2013), edited by Ira Berlin, Leslie Rowland, and others. We were just beginning to reap the reward of prize-winning studies by Deborah Grey White, Jacqueline Jones, Leslie Schwalm, and Jean Fagan Yellin. The list of creative scholarly contributions has multiplied exponentially in the past two decades and is more of a cloud source than a list.[85]

African American women had a special stake in the struggle, as they rightly perceived of the Civil War as a battle for black liberation: war, the dizzying carousel, and, emancipation, the brass ring. Their moving roles in the Civil War demand our attention. Too many enslaved women found war a sheer hell, as did the Missouri wife who wrote her husband: "They are treating me worse and worse every day. Our child cries for you. Send me some money as soon as you can for me and my child are almost naked."[86]

In the anthology *Battle Scars: Gender and Sexuality in the American Civil War* (2006), which I coedited with Nina Silber, Jim Downs began his essay with an anonymous black woman, lying half-dead in a ditch, found by a Freedmen's Bureau official in 1866. She was brought into camp without identification, metaphorically lost, literally blind—just another of war's victims. He confronts us with such neglected victims of war, too long denied their rightful place as historical actors because of their color, because of their sex, because of a cause not lost but cruelly postponed. These nameless women, restless in their unmarked graves, cannot be redeemed by any Mammy monument.

These anonymous sisters demand to be given their due, and a talented army of scholars seems to be crossing that field in twenty-first-century Civil War studies. A new literature on black men and women, enslaved and liberated, emerges with the publication and reprinting of powerful memoirs such as Harriet Jacobs's *Incidents in the Life of a Slave Girl*, Carol Ione's *Pride of Family: Four Generations of American Women of Color*, Pauli Murray's *Proud Shoes*, and, more recently, Carla Peterson's *Black Gotham: A Family History of African Americans in Nineteenth Century New York City*. Harriet Jacobs published her own story (under a pseudonym) in 1863, chronicling her life in slavery and freedom.[87] Pauli Murray tells the powerful story of her North Carolina forebears, including Cornelia Smith, an enslaved woman who bore mixed-race children.[88] Ione sketches the lives of her free black ancestors in antebellum South Carolina, including William Rollin, who sided with the Confederacy during the Civil War. His daughter Frances Rollin became a writer, teacher, and political activist for black rights. Rollin may have been the first African American woman to publish a volume of history, *Life and Public Services of Martin R. Delany* (1868), written under the name of "Frank" A. Rollin.[89] Peterson shares the story of Maritcha Lyons, one of New York's elite black abolitionists who agitated to improve the lot of fellow African Americans.[90] Despite these vivid portraits of real African American women during the Civil War, fiction continues to trump facts.

After the Civil War, southern propaganda became so popular that northern writers joined the stampede to cash in on its popularity. Kathryn Floyd Dana lived in New York but wrote under the name of Olive A. Wadsworth. (She signed her letters "O. A. W." which was short for "only a woman.") Her southern vernacular tales, such as "Aunt Rosy's Chest" (1872), reflected the craze for literary blackface. Another local colorist, Sherwood Bonner, had more authentic roots. She spent her childhood and youth in Holly Springs, Mississippi, before taking the long train to Boston to reinvent herself as a lady author. Once settled in Massachusetts, Bonner chose to sell stories of the South to support herself as a "local colorist."[91]

Whites invented tales of Mammies and filtered them through the lens of romanticized fiction, what I suggest might be called "Confederate porn" (more for the fact that it remained *hidden* in polite company, rather than for what it contained.) These products of yore are not being replaced fast enough by the stories of the flesh-and-blood women whose dramatic transformations from enslavement to emancipation demand more attention.

In 2009, the *New York Times* featured the story of a six-year-old "negro girl Melvinia," born in South Carolina and bequeathed by her owner, David Patterson, to his wife Ruth. When Ruth died in 1852, Melvinia (known as Mattie) went to live with Ruth's daughter Christianne Shields. Living in rural Georgia, near Atlanta, Mattie was illiterate and like most women of her generation struggled against incredible odds to survive. In 1870, she appears in the census with four children, more than one of whom may have been fathered by a son of her former master, Charles

Shields, or by Shields himself. Mattie worked as a maid, a washerwoman, and a farmhand, and lived a hard life before her death in the 1930s—no fictional Mammy she.

One of Melvinia's sons, Dolphus Shields, did learn to read and write, and by 1900 he was listed in the Birmingham, Alabama, census as owning his own home. He and his first wife Alice had a son named Robert. Robert married Annie, and she bore him two children. Robert drops out of the record, but following his disappearance, we know that his wife Annie moved to Chicago during the Great Migration.[92] Their son, Purnell Nathaniel Shields, married a nurse, and together, they had eight children. The granddaughter of this Chicago couple, Michelle Obama, moved into the White House as First Lady in 2009.[93]

There are many more stories, just as compelling, about the lives of black women and men who have been left on the sidelines of history, their tracks nearly erased.[94] Their recovery is an important aspect of southern women's history, as is the dismantling of the Mammy. These are interlocking projects—the recovery of the stories of real African Americans from the Civil War era, and the interrogation of the roots of mythmaking and its effect on our present.

In many ways, the Mammy is a bedrock of contradiction. She was supposed to be the one to heal her white charges, who as children were wholly dependent on this figure for nurture and as adults could only fully realize their humanity with appreciation of her special place in their psyche. This was a mantra that developed in the Reconstruction era, as when E. A. Pollard, the Virginian who published *The Lost Cause* in 1866, waxed romantically about Aunt Debby, his eyes "tenderly filled with tears" as he recalled the image "of that dear old slave."[95] Pollard's romantic racialism is still at the core of modern debates over southern women's race relations. The issue imploded in the headlines much more recently with the depictions projected in Kathryn Stockett's 2009 novel, *The Help,* and the 2011 film based on it.[96]

Film has played a special place in fixing the image of the Mammy in the American imagination. Silent films such as *The Slave* (1905) and *The Nigger* (1915) kept racist stereotyping vivid in a new medium. D. W. Griffith's premiere of *Birth of a Nation,* the most technically advanced and ideologically retrograde American film ever produced, was busy with so many stereotypes that black women seem lost in the shuffle. Jennie Lee was cast in the role of Mammy and used to comic effect, including slapstick. Humor injected at the black woman's expense becomes a running theme for this stock character, who one critic dubbed as "Sassy Mammy." More than one black actress struggled to invert the sass into her own brand of resistance. It was in this role that Hattie McDaniel earned her reputation as a reliable actress—playing Mammy. She delivered a string of feisty screen appearances, including in *The Little Colonel* (1935), *Alice Adams* (1935), and *Saratoga* (1937), before her Oscar-winning performance in *Gone With the Wind* (1939).

These women who might sass owners and employers, who asserted themselves on-screen, do not provide us with as vibrant a record as is revealed in the Freedmen's Bureau papers. Consider the ex-slave Peggy, who challenged rice planter and former owner Charles Manigault when he came with wagons to strip the cabins of their furniture. "Placing her arms akimbo," [she] said "she would go off to the Provost Marshal in town & stop our unlawful proceedings with her property in their own homes."[97] She and her children were shortly thereafter evicted. When Peggy died three months later, it was a sad end to a defiant woman.[98]

Contrast this with the rhetoric, more than half a century later, of white southern congressmen suggesting that the government fund a statue in the nation's capital "in memory of the faithful slave mammies of the South."[99] This was in no way meant as a progressive tribute to African Americans; these same politicians allowed a filibuster to defeat an antilynching bill. African Americans raised strategic protests, and one black paper argued that a statue of a "White Daddy" might be included, with the Mammy looking on helplessly as he assaulted a young black woman.

Several models were proposed, and an image of a Mammy with an infant (presumably white) at her breast won the contest.[100] The massive outpouring of protest from African Americans derailed this memorial scheme; Mary Church Terrell suggested that prayer might insure "lightning will strike it and the heavenly elements will send it crashing to the ground." This cataclysm never took place, but it mobilized a generation to agitate against these assaults.

Nearly a century ago, white activist Lilly Hammond issued a call, titled "Bury the Mammy": "Her being dead is no bar to affection; but it certainly should bar a daily association with her corpse which threatens the corruption of sentiment into sentimentality. Wrenched from a past environment to which alone she belonged, and set up fetish like, in a life in which she can have no rightful place, she expresses an attitude of the white mind which is at once ludicrous, tragic, and fraught with future peril."[101] Hammond was unable to move other white progressives of her generation—women in the modern South who might have rallied to condemn racist caricatures that condemned black and white to conform to inauthenticity.

Mammy may seem to have nine lives, but hopefully at least eight of them are gone. She was just wallpaper in Tom and Jerry cartoons, and then she morphed into a maid with *Beulah* (both on radio and television) in the 1950s. Some suggest that the Mammy has been magically shape-shifted into the Angry Black Woman, the Welfare Queen, or any number of contemporary caricatures that demonized black women at the end of the last century.

None of the current generation of African American achievers, from Oprah Winfrey to Condoleezza Rice to Toni Morrison, has fully escaped these epithets. Perhaps the first African American First Lady, Michelle Obama, can coax permanent changes. She has been one of the most admired women in twenty-first-century America, an emblematic black woman whose reputation and reach contributes to altered agendas. But clinging to stereotypes and legends—like pretending Johnny Appleseed was an environmental activist and Pocahontas's marriage to John Rolfe was a love story—is a national obsession. We live in a world turned up-side down by biomyths, but we also live an age with increasing access to tools we can use to torpedo such fabrications.

Can Mammy be ushered off stage, or at least reduced to an extra in the background? Critics suggest she was updated and given a star turn with the 2009 best-selling novel, *The Help*. This modern Mammy went global on-screen, with the Oscar-winning performance by Octavia Spencer in the 2011 film version of the book. The lead actress in the film, Viola Davis, might have put portrayals of maids behind her, but she is still on the warpath against limited access to potentially award-winning roles: "And let me tell you something: The only thing that separates women of color from anyone else is opportunity."[102]

Scholars of African American studies recognize that campaigns against the Mammy are only one aspect of the larger enterprise to recast the image of black women in America, to acknowledge their historical pasts and foremothers' considerable achievements.[103] Artist Kara Walker has produced a string of powerful cultural interventions with her films and art installations, most especially her much publicized 2014 installation in New York (Williamsburg) of a colossal Mammy sphinx—thirty-five feet tall and seventy-five feet long—made of sugar. The curatorial statement describes: "Walker's sphinx is a hybrid of two distinct racist stereotypes of the black female: She has the head of a kerchief-wearing black female, referencing the mythic caretaker of the domestic needs of white families, especially the raising and care of their children, but her body is a veritable caricature of the overly sexualized black woman, with prominent breasts, enormous buttocks, and protruding vulva that is quite visible from the back."[104]

At the behest of Creative Time Kara E. Walker has confected:

## A SUBTLETY
### OR THE *MARVELOUS SUGAR BABY*

an Homage to the unpaid and overworked Artisans who have refined
our Sweet tastes from the cane fields to the Kitchens of the New World
on the Occasion of the demolition of the Domino Sugar Refining Plant[105]

As critic Gloria Malone suggests, "The sugar sphinx was a prodigious representation of the many Black women who worked under deadly and forced labor conditions all while remaining nameless and barely known."[106] To find out their names and insert them into the narrative remains a goal for several larger historical missions.

Mammy is being dismantled by new tools, even as she continues to haunt. She is being systematically diminished by a vast army of documented lives, lives emerging from the shadows; in her place are women reconstructed by sharp-eyed scholars rather than misty-eyed memoirists.

Many of these recovered subjects were not always agents of their own destinies, but at least their rebirths were midwifed by scholars dedicated to reclamation. Heroic recovery of women might occur even without names, as scholarly reconstructions of black women's lives by Jim Downs and Thavolia Glymph demonstrate.

Simultaneously, there are movements kicking into high gear and disturbances in the field which signal a revolutionary reordering of priorities: people over property, personal as political. There are a range of slogans to reflect change afoot. Mammy will become persona non grata, losing her status, her homeland, her appeal, even as a relic. As boundaries are redrawn, a phalanx of black women of the nineteenth-century South will replace her. She may never disappear, but she can certainly fade to a faint outline of her former self. As she becomes less visible, other, more representative images are replacing her, while invisibility is tackled.

By forcing media to revisit the malignant neglect of black women, contemporary activists are carving out a new space for public discourse on race, gender, and sex. The most devastating campaigns relating to this larger arc of black struggle is the "#SayHerName" initiative.[107] A founding statement suggests: "Say Her Name is intended to serve as a resource for the media, organizers, researchers, policy makers, and other stakeholders to better understand and address Black women's experiences of profiling and policing."[108]

But #SayHerName is much more. Yes, it may raise awareness about the significance of women of color in the American justice system (as legal and political priorities interlock to perpetuate justice for "just-us-men"), but the initiative targets larger goals. It makes reclamation a means of empowerment for those unnamed and for those demanding the naming. These women will not be appeased by a body count in a narrative of black murder in America today. The demands for memory and media synergize within the next round of scholarly revisionism. Historians and sister scholars will create new waves, currents, and storms—sending Mammy adrift. A new generation is creating clouds, posts, and hashtags signaling not just voices for inclusion, but their own voice. Tell her story, say her name, and in the retelling, be reborn, with both a future and a past.

# NOTES

~~~~~~

## INTRODUCTION

1. See http://opinionator.blogs.nytimes.com/2011/09/20/recounting-the-dead/#more-105317; see also J. David Hacker, "A Census-Based Count of the Civil War Dead" in *Civil War History* 57, no. 4 (December 2011).

2. http://discovere.binghamton.edu/news/civilwar-3826.html.

3. Ibid.

4. Ibid.

5. www.slate.com/articles/arts/culturebox/2011/06/thanks_a_lot_ken_burns.single.html.

6. Catherine Clinton, "Noble Women as Well," in Robert Brent Toplin, ed., *Ken Burns's The Civil War: Historians Respond* (New York: Oxford University Press, 1996).

7. Although recent prohibitions concerning the Confederate flag may dampen this market—or raise the price, if they become collectors' items.

8. Coedited with Nina Silber.

9. See Catherine Clinton, ed., *Reminiscences of My Life in Camp: An African American Woman's Civil War Memoir,* by Susie King Taylor (Athens: University of Georgia Press, 2006), and Catherine Clinton, *Civil War Stories,* Averitt Lecture Series, Georgia Southern University (Athens: University of Georgia Press, 1998).

10. See http://rebeldocumentary.com/about/the-film.

11. It is wonderful to see Carol Bleser's significant series, Women's Diaries and Letters of the South, continue at the University of South Carolina Press under the leadership of Melissa Walker and Giselle Roberts. These and other primary source projects stimulate rising generations of scholars in this field.

## CHAPTER ONE

1. Catherine Clinton, *Tara Revisited: Women, War, and the Plantation Legend* (New York: Abbeville, 1995); see chap. 5, "The Cult of Sacrifice."

2. I thank the anonymous reader at LSU Press who generously provided critical suggestions, including this particular image of Chesnut.

3. Clinton, *Tara Revisited,* 64.

4. Ibid.

5. See Leigh Fought, *Southern Womanhood and Slavery: A Biography of Louisa S. McCord, 1810–1879* (Columbia: University of Missouri Press, 2003), and Drew Gilpin Faust, introduction to *Macaria,* by Augusta Jane Evans (Baton Rouge: LSU Press, 1992).

6. See Mary Elizabeth Massey, *Bonnet Brigades: American Women and the Civil War* (New York: Knopf, 1966), and "Historians Forum: Bonnet Brigades at Fifty: Reflections on Mary Elizabeth Massey and Gender in Civil War History," *Civil War History* 61, no. 4 (December 2015).

7. Stephanie McCurry, *Confederate Reckoning: Politics and Power in the Civil War South* (Cambridge, MA: Harvard University Press, 2010), 85.

8. Daniel Stowell, "A Family of Women and Children," in *Southern Families at War: Loyalty and Conflict in the Civil War South,* ed. Catherine Clinton (New York: Oxford University Press, 2000), 166.

9. See Anne Firor Scott, *The Southern Lady: From Pedestal to Politics, 1830–1930* (Chicago: University of Chicago Press, 1970). My own work suggests that more women continued the precedent set by plantation mistresses to manage households and estates (in the absence of husbands, brothers, or fathers), and this role was altered dramatically as they contemplated that these male family members might *never* return, so the burdens were more psychological than managerial. I argue that the majority were skilled at the job of keeping the home fires burning even before war erupted. See Catherine Clinton, *The Plantation Mistress: Woman's World in the Old South* (New York: Pantheon, 1982). This view is compatible with the findings of Deborah Gray White, *Aren't I a Woman: Female Slaves in the Plantation South* (New York: W. W. Norton, 1985), among others. Interpretations over the meaning of planters' wives' roles—in terms of labor, management, and impact on the plantation economy and slaveholding—continues a topic of heated debate.

10. Drew Gilpin Faust, *Mothers of Invention: Women of the Slaveholding South in the American Civil War* (Chapel Hill: University of North Carolina Press, 1996), 111.

11. Sallie Moore, *Memories of a Long Life in Virginia* (Staunton, VA: McClure Co., 1920), 70.

12. Louisa Henry to her mother, March 28, 1864, Arcadia, Mississippi, Boddie Family Papers, Mississippi State Archives, Jackson, MS.

13. Quoted by Stephanie McCurry in "Steel Magnolias," a review of Faust's *Mothers of Invention,* and LeeAnn Whites's *The Civil War as a Crisis in Gender,* in the *Women's Review of Books* 14, no. 6 (March 1997): 13–14.

14. See LeeAnn Whites and Alecia P. Long, eds., *Occupied Women: Gender, Military Occupation, and the American Civil War* (Baton Rouge: LSU Press, 2009).

15. Mary Ann Huff, "The Role of Women in Confederate Georgia" (master's thesis, Vanderbilt University, 1967), 72.

16. Clinton, *Tara Revisited,* 123.

17. Faust, *Mothers of Invention,* 8.

18. Ibid., 3.

19. Ibid., 42.

20. Her claim remains relatively unchallenged and is bolstered by evidence drawn from several hundred manuscript collections.

21. See newer interpretations of Confederate women which demonstrate alternate views, for example, Kristen Cree Brill, "Rewriting Southern Womanhood in the American Civil War" (PhD diss., University of Cambridge, 2013).

22. For perhaps the most explicit refutation of this thesis, see Gary Gallagher's *The Confederate War* (Cambridge, MA: Harvard University Press, 1999).

23. See, e.g., Victoria Bynum's *The Long Shadow of the Civil War: Southern Dissent and Its Legacies* (Chapel Hill: University of North Carolina Press, 2010), which illuminates the ways in which defiance also shaped the South during the Rebellion.

24. See Elizabeth Fox-Genovese, *Within the Plantation Household: Black and White Women of the Old South* (Chapel Hill: University of North Carolina Press, 1988). Stephanie McCurry's *Masters of Small Worlds: Yeoman Households, Gender Relations, and the Political Culture of the Antebellum South Carolina Low Country* (New York: Oxford University Press, 1995) suggests that yeomen's rule over their own households was a primary source of their power within the Old South. See also "The Civil War as a Household War," a forthcoming anthology edited by Lisa Tendrich Frank and LeeAnn Whites.

25. McCurry, *Confederate Reckoning,* expands and extends a thesis developed by Emory M. Thomas more than forty years ago in *The Confederacy as a Revolutionary Experience* (1970; reprint, Columbia: University of South Carolina Press, 1992).

26. Several critics have taken McCurry to task for not defining more clearly "the state" in her book: Does she mean an individual state, such as South Carolina, or the Confederate national government or some other interpretation? Lockean? Foucault's proclamation of the state as abstraction? She is pointedly fluid but always purposeful in arguing her case. The ambiguity of her use of the term "state" (as well as "project" and "citizen") allows her an elasticity that is both frustrating and admirable.

27. McCurry, *Confederate Reckoning,* 203.

28. Ibid., 156.

29. See Michael B. Chesson, "Harlots or Heroines," *Virginia Magazine of Biography and History* 92 (1984), and also Catherine Clinton, "'Public Women' and Sexual Politics During the Civil War," in Catherine Clinton and Nina Silber, eds., *Battle Scars: Gender and Sexuality in the American Civil War* (New York: Oxford University Press, 2006).

30. Katharine Jones, *Ladies of Richmond* (Indianapolis: Bobbs-Merrill, 1962), 156.

31. See Catherine Clinton, "Reading Between the Lines: Newspapers and Women in Confederate Richmond," *Atlanta History* 42, no. 1–2 (Spring–Summer 1998).

32. See Catherine Clinton and Nina Silber, eds., *Divided Houses: Gender and the Civil War* (New York: Oxford University Press, 1995), *particularly* the bibliography, and Clinton and Silber, *Battle Scars*.

33. Leslie Schwalm's *A Hard Fight for We: Women's Transition from Slavery to Freedom in South Carolina* (Champaign-Urbana: University of Illinois Press, 1997) was a pioneering volume, followed shortly thereafter by Noralee Frankel's *Freedom's Women: Black Women and Families in Civil War Era Mississippi* (Bloomington: Indiana University Press, 1999). Ella Forbes's rarely cited *African American Women During the Civil War* (New York: Routledge, 1998) fell far short of a comprehensive work, and the field lay fallow until Thavolia Glymph's *Out of the House of Bondage: The Transformation of the Plantation Household* (Cambridge: Cambridge University Press, 2008) appeared, the first substantial volume on this topic.

34. William B. Rogers and Terese Martyn, "A Consensus at Last: American Civil War Texts and the Topics That Dominate the College Classroom," *History Teacher* 41, no. 4 (Aug. 2008): 519–30.

35. An all too common conflation! But the authors noted that the inclusion of Deborah Gray White's *Aren't I a Woman: Female Slaves in the Plantation South* allowed some instructors to cover both topics simultaneously.

36. Rogers and Martyn, "A Consensus at Last," 528.

37. Edmund Wilson, *Patriotic Gore: Studies in the Literature of the American Civil War* (New York: Oxford University Press, 1962); Anne Goodwyn Jones, *Tomorrow Is Another Day: The Woman Writer in the South, 1859–1936* (Baton Rouge: LSU Press, 1981); Sarah Gardner, *Blood and Irony: Southern White Women's Narratives of the Civil War, 1861–1937* (Chapel Hill: University of North Carolina, 2003); and Caroline Janney *Remembering the Civil War: Reunion and the Limits of Reconciliation* (Chapel Hill: University of North Carolina, 2013).

38. Evans to Mr. Jabez Lamar Monroe Curry, July 15, 1863, in Rebecca Grant Sexton, ed., *A Southern Woman of Letters: The Correspondence of Augusta Jane Evans Wilson* (Columbia: University of South Carolina Press, 2002).

39. Elizabeth Moss, *Domestic Novelists in the Old South: Defenders of Southern Culture* (Baton Rouge: LSU Press, 1992), 8.

40. Sexton, *A Southern Woman of Letters*, 131.

41. Moss, *Domestic Novelists in the Old South*, 5.

42. See, in particular, the literature examining the Fugitives movement and Twelve Southerners, *I'll Take My Stand: The South and the Agrarian Tradition* (1920; reprint, Baton Rouge: LSU Press, 2006).

43. Rollin G. Osterweis, *The Myth of the Lost Cause, 1865–1900* (Hamden, CT: Archon Books, 1973); Charles Reagan Wilson, *Baptized in Blood: The Religion of the Lost Cause, 1865–1920* (Athens: University of Georgia Press, 1980); Gaines M. Foster, *Ghosts of the Confederacy: Defeat, the Lost Cause, and the Emergence of the New South, 1865–1913* (New York: Oxford University Press, 1987); John Coski, *The Confederate Battle Flag: America's Most Embattled Emblem* (Cambridge: Harvard University Press, 2005); Cynthia Mills and

Pamela H. Simpson, eds., *Monuments to the Lost Cause: Women, Art, and the Landscapes of Southern Memory* (Knoxville: University of Tennessee Press, 2003); Karen Cox, *Dixie's Daughters: The United Daughters of the Confederacy and the Preservation of Confederate Culture* (Gainesville: University Press of Florida, 2003); W. Scott Poole, *Never Surrender: Confederate Memory and Conservatism in the South Carolina Upcountry* (Athens: University of Georgia, 2004); W. Fitzhugh Brundage, *Where These Memories Grow: History, Memory, and Southern Identity* (Chapel Hill: University of North Carolina Press, 2000). See also Alice Fahs and Joan Waugh, eds., *The Memory of the Civil War in American Culture* (Chapel Hill: University of North Carolina Press, 2004); Gary W. Gallagher and Alan T. Nolan, eds., *The Myth of the Lost Cause and Civil War History* (Bloomington: Indiana University Press, 2000); David Goldfield, *Still Fighting the Civil War: The American South and Southern History* (Baton Rouge: LSU Press, 2002); and Nina Silber, *The Romance of Reunion: Northerners and the South, 1865–1900* (Chapel Hill: University of North Carolina Press, 1993).

44. Faust, *Mothers of Invention,* and McCurry, *Confederate Reckonings,* as well as Glymph, *Out of the House of Bondage;* LeeAnn Whites, *The Civil War as a Crisis in Gender: Augusta, Georgia, 1860–1890* (Athens: University of Georgia Press, 1995); Nell Irwin Painter, introduction to Virginia Ingraham Burr, ed., *The Secret Eye: The Journal of Ella Gertrude Clanton Thomas, 1848–1889* (Chapel Hill: University of North Carolina, 1990); Laura F. Edwards, *Scarlett Doesn't Live Here Anymore: Southern Women in the Civil War Era* (Urbana-Champaign: University of Illinois Press, 2004); Julia Stern, *Mary Chesnut's Civil War Epic* (Chicago: University of Chicago, 2010); Mary De Credico, *Mary Boykin Chesnut: A Confederate Woman's Life* (Lanham, MD: Rowman and Littlefield, 2002); Elisabeth S. Muhlenfield, *Mary Boykin Chesnut: A Biography* (Baton Rouge: LSU Press, 1992); Lisa Tendrich Frank, *The Civilian War: Confederate Women and Union Soldiers during Sherman's March* (Baton Rouge: LSU Press, 2015); Giselle Roberts, *The Confederate Belle* (Columbia: University of Missouri Press, 2003); Victoria Ott, *Confederate Daughters: Coming of Age During the Civil War* (Carbondale: Southern Illinois University Press, 2008).

45. I wish to thank the Walter Lynwood Fleming lectures for the invitation to revisit the topic of southern women. The folks in Baton Rouge were very hospitable, and I appreciated, in particular, Gaines Foster's collegiality during my preparations for the lectures and Rand Dotson's kindness during the run up to publication.

46. See introduction to Catherine Clinton, ed., *Reminiscences of My Life in Camp: An African American Woman's Civil War Memoir,* by Susie King Taylor (Athens: University of Georgia Press, 2006), and "Legendary Valor: South Carolina Women Reconstruct the War," chap. 3 of Catherine Clinton, *Civil War Stories* (Athens: University of Georgia Press, 1998).

47. Loreta Janeta Velazquez, *The Woman in Battle: A Narrative of the Exploits, Adventures, and Travels of Madame Loreta Janeta Velazquez* (Richmond, VA: Dustin, Gilman and Co., 1876), 224.

48. Carl Weinberg, "Judith Carter Henry at the Crossroads," *OAH Magazine of History,* 26, no. 2 (April 2012).

49. Mary Ann Loughborough, *My Cave Life in Vicksburg* (New York: D. Appleton and Co., 1864).

50. Ibid., 56.

51. Ibid., 115.

52. John Seymour Erwin, *Like Some Green Laurel: Letters of Margaret Johnson Erwin, 1821–1863* (Baton Rouge: LSU Press, 1981), 121, 127. She also feared rumors of cholera.

53. Ibid., 127.

54. Ibid., 129.

55. Ibid., 133.

56. To this day, I remain grateful to the Virginia Historical Society archivist who, as I found myself weeping—lost in one of the many sad stories encountered in archives—most gently asked me not to cry on the documents.

57. Mary Vaughn to her sister, February 22, 1862, Sunnyside, Boddie Family Papers, Mississippi State Archives.

58. Besides the nearly one hundred edited volumes still in print—and nearly another hundred out of print but still available—there are at least a dozen critical studies of Confederate women: a bounty of literature is available. But slowly, through the hard work of recovery, the voices of formerly enslaved women are emerging as well: Dorothy Sterling's pioneering anthology, *We Are Your Sisters: Black Women in the Nineteenth Century* (New York: W. W. Norton, 1984) is but one of a handful of important works in the past quarter century expanding our appreciation of African American women during the Civil War.

59. She goes on to modestly insist that she is "painfully aware that the hallowed mantle of Xenophon and Tacitus would not fit my shoulders" (Augusta Jane Evans to Alexander Stephens, November 29, 1865, in Sexton, *A Southern Woman of Letters,* 130).

60. The southern quill could not be stilled, which is what gave Chesnut such hope during her lifetime. During the period 1865 to 1885, most southern authors focused on the idealization of the antebellum period and underscored the dark age enforced by surrender. A steady stream of romantic, sentimentalized portraits appeared. Once southerners and northerners went to war on the same side—in the brief but "splendid little war" with Spain between April and August in 1898—the full cycle of military reconciliation was completed. War memoirs became bestselling books, including Confederate reminiscences—especially those penned by women.

61. See Ellwood Parry, *The Image of the Indian and the Black Man in American Art, 1590–1900* (New York: George Braziller, 1974).

62. Drew Gilpin Faust, "Altars of Sacrifice: Confederate Women and the Narratives of War," in Clinton and Silber, *Divided Houses.*

63. See Karen Cox, *Dixie's Daughters: The United Daughters of the Confederacy and the Preservation of Confederate Culture* (Gainesville: University Press of Florida, 2003); Cynthia Mills, *Beyond Grief: Sculpture and Wonder in the Gilded Age Cemetery* (Washington: Smithsonian Press, 2015); Mills and Simpson, *Monuments to the Lost Cause,* and, most recently,

Caroline Janney, *Burying the Dead but Not the Past: Ladies' Memorial Associations and the Lost Cause* (Chapel Hill: University of North Carolina Press, 2011).

64. Much of this memorialization is under fire and may disappear during contemporary campaigns to strip public space of "hurtful" or "offensive" monuments erected as part of a project of perpetuating white supremacy in the wake of emancipation and campaigns for African American civil rights.

65. Anne Bradstreet, "Prologue," www.poetryfoundation.org/poem/172961.

66. Several of my examples are drawn from Louisiana in deference to the public audience at LSU, where the lectures were first delivered in the winter of 2012–13.

67. Walter Sullivan, *The War the Women Lived: Female Voices from the Confederate South* (Nashville: J. S. Sanders and Co., 1995), 69; Sarah Morgan Dawson, *A Confederate Girl's Diary,* with an introduction by Warrington Dawson (Boston: Houghton Mifflin Co., 1913), 247.

68. In 1960, James I. Robertson Jr. edited a new edition (Bloomington: Indiana University Press, 1960), and Charles East included an excellent introduction in his authoritative edition entitled *The Civil War Diary of Sarah Morgan* (Athens: University of Georgia, 1991).

69. In 1955, a new edition of the book enhanced its value and expanded its reputation; forty years later it was reprinted with a new introduction by Drew Gilpin Faust, gaining an even wider audience. John Q. Anderson, ed., *Brokenburn: The Journal of Kate Stone, 1861–1868* (Baton Rouge: LSU Press, 1955), xi.

70. Ibid., 17.

71. Ibid., 183.

72. Ibid., 8.

73. March 20, 1863, ibid., 181.

74. By contrast, although clearly unhappy with family burdens, Lizzie Neblett was more stoic about her lot. In March 1864, she wrote, "You speak of my self-sacrifices, I admit, my life has been full of such, but don't make a virtue of what was a necessity. Woman was made for such things, and when she tries to evade them is only kicking against the thorns." See Erika R. Murr, ed., *A Rebel Wife in Texas: The Diary and Letters of Elizabeth Scott Neblett, 1852–1864* (Baton Rouge: LSU Press, 2001), 20. Faust portrays Neblett as more bitter, but there is a balance in Murr's portrait—so perhaps different scholars read different things into such a document.

75. Anderson, *Brokenburn,* 340.

76. In her later years, she became active in the United Daughters of the Confederacy and in local book and literary clubs. Kate Stone died in 1907, at the age of sixty-five.

77. Two children predeceased her.

78. Anderson, *Brokenburn,* 607.

79. *Confederate Scrapbook* (Richmond, VA: J. L. Hill, 1893), 56. Available at Special Collections, Lipscomb Library, Randolph College, Lynchburg, Virginia.

80. See Clinton, *Tara Revisited,* 132.

81. Joan Cashin, *First Lady of the Confederacy: Varina Davis's Civil War* (Cambridge: Harvard University Press, 2009).

82. Hudson Strode, *Jefferson Davis: Confederate President* (New York: Harcourt, 1959), 2:34.

83. Ibid.

84. See Heath Lee, *Winnie Davis: Daughter of the Lost Cause* (Lincoln, NE: Potomac Books, 2014).

85. Lesley J. Gordon, *General George E. Pickett in Life and Legend* (Chapel Hill: University of North Carolina Press, 1998), 171.

86. Gordon, *General George E. Pickett*, 173.

87. Clinton, *Tara Revisited*, 203–4.

88. See Joel Chandler Harris, *Uncle Remus, His Songs and His Sayings: The Folk-Lore of the Old Plantation* (New York: D. Appleton, 1881), and Thomas Nelson Page, *In Ole Virginia; Or, Marse Chan, and Other Stories* (New York: Scribner, 1890).

89. Clinton, *Tara Revisited*, 202.

90. Capt. W. R. Bond, *Pickett or Pettigrew? North Carolina at Gettysburg: A Historical Monograph* (1888; reprint, Scotland Neck, NC: W. L. L. Hall, 1901), 8.

91. Ibid., 91. See also Frank Moore, ed., *The Rebellion Record: A Diary of American Events*, 11 vols. (New York: G. P. Putnam, 1861–68).

92. LaSalle Corbell Pickett, *Pickett and His Men* (Atlanta: Foote and Davies, 1899); Gallagher and Nolan, *The Myth of the Lost Cause*, 172.

93. Gary Gallagher, "A Widow and Her Soldier: LaSalle Corbell Pickett as Author of the George E. Pickett Letters," *Virginia Magazine of History and Biography* 94, no. 3 (July 1986), 329–34.

94. Clinton, *Tara Revisited*, 183.

95. Woodrow Wilson, "Address at Gettysburg," July 4, 1913, www. presidency.ucsb.edu/ws/?pid=65370.

96. See David Blight, *Race and Reunion: The Civil War in American Memory* (Cambridge: Harvard University Press, 2001).

97. All Chesnut quotes are taken from Catherine Clinton, ed., *Mary Chesnut's Diary* (New York: Penguin, 2011), 68.

98. Ibid., 170.

99. See Stern, *Mary Chesnut's Civil War Epic*, and Muhlenfeld, *Mary Boykin Chesnut*, and also consult C. Vann Woodward's *Mary Chesnut's Civil War* (New Haven, CT: Yale University Press, 1981) for Chesnut's editorial interventions.

100. Ibid., 4.

101. Muhlenfeld, *Mary Boykin Chesnut*, 223.

102. Clinton, *Mary Chesnut's Diary*, 258.

103. Ibid., 397.

104. Ibid., 200.

105. Ibid., 164.

106. Ibid., 335.

107. Ibid., 3.

108. Ibid., 297, 60, 9.

109. Ibid., 8, 151.

110. Isabella D. Martin and Myrta Lockett Avary, eds., *A Diary from Dixie,* by Mary Chesnut (New York: D. Appleton, 1905), xiv.

111. Clinton, *Mary Chesnut's Diary,* 114–16.

112. Ibid., 133.

113. Ibid., 127, 26.

114. Ibid., 141.

115. Muhlenfeld, *Mary Boykin Chesnut,* 203.

116. Clinton, *Mary Chesnut's Diary,* 12.

117. Ibid., 33, 283, 332.

118. Ibid., 332.

119. Ibid., 147, 301, 317–18, 346.

120. Avary and Martin, *A Diary From Dixie,* xxii.

121. Following some scholars' criticism of Woodward's editorial choices, he coedited an edition of Chesnut's wartime journal entries: C. Vann Woodward and Elisabeth Muhlenfeld, eds., *The Private Mary Chesnut: The Unpublished Civil War Diaries* (New York: Oxford University Press, 1984). Muhlenfeld has also edited two of Chesnut's previously unpublished fictional works: *Two Novels: The Captain and the Colonel / Two Years, or, The Way We Lived Then* (Charlottesville: University of Virginia Press, 2002).

122. Clinton, *Mary Chesnut's Diary,* xxii–xxiii.

123. See Catherine Clinton, "Queen Bee of the Confederacy," *New York Times,* May 26, 2011, http://opinionator.blogs.nytimes.com/2011/05/26/queen-bee-of-the-confederacy/?_r=0.

CHAPTER TWO

1. See Maria Agui Carter, *Rebel!* (Iguana Films, 2013); Elizabeth Leonard, *All the Daring of the Soldier: Women of the Civil War Armies* (New York: W. W. Norton, 1999); DeAnne Blanton and Lauren M. Cook, *They Fought Like Demons: Women Soldiers in the American Civil War* (Baton Rouge: LSU Press, 2002).

2. William C. Davis has been working on a book-length manuscript that he promises will expose Velazquez and her memoir as "fake." He has been advertising this for some time; see "The Lies of Loreta Velasquez," Louisville Civil War Round Table, May 11, 2013; "Who Was Loreta Velasquez?" Raleigh Civil War Round Table, April 2014; and http://deborahkalbbooks.blogspot.com/2015/06/q-with-william-c-davis.html.

3. Loreta Janeta Velazquez, *The Woman in Battle: A Narrative of the Exploits, Adventures, and Travels of Madame Loreta Janeta Velazquez* (Richmond, VA: Dustin, Gilman and Co., 1876), 136.

4. Ibid., 60.

5. Ibid., 37, 131.

6. See, e.g., Blanton and Cook, *They Fought Like Demons*, 25–26.

7. Velasquez, *The Woman in Battle*, 42.

8. Ibid., 45.

9. Ibid., 340.

10. Ibid., 63.

11. Ibid., 100.

12. Ibid., 128.

13. Ibid., 41, 146.

14. Ibid., 125.

15. Ibid., 129.

16. Headline, *Lynchburg Daily Virginian*, July 2, 1863.

17. Ibid., 130.

18. Ibid., 301, 536.

19. Ibid. 34.

20. Ibid., 38.

21. See Gary W. Gallagher, "Jubal A. Early, the Lost Cause, and Civil War History: A Persistent Legacy," in Gary W. Gallagher and Alan T. Nolan, eds., *The Myth of the Lost Cause and Civil War History* (Bloomington: Indiana University Press, 2000).

22. http://deborahkalbbooks.blogspot.com/2015/06/q-with-william-c-davis.html.

23. Ibid.

24. See Carter, *Rebel!*

25. See Catherine Clinton, "'Public Women' and Sexual Politics during the American Civil War," in Catherine Clinton and Nina Silber, eds., *Battle Scars: Gender and Sexuality in the American Civil War* (New York: Oxford University Press, 2006).

26. Anya Jabour, *Scarlett's Sisters: Young Women in the Old South* (Chapel Hill: University of North Carolina Press, 2009).

27. See Catherine Clinton, *The Plantation Mistress: Woman's World in the Old South* (New York: Pantheon, 1982), chap. 6, "The Fallen Woman."

28. Betina Entzminger, *The Belle Gone Bad: White Southern Women Writers and the Dark Seductress* (Baton Rouge: LSU Press, 2002), 3.

29. Clinton, *Plantation Mistress*, chap. 11, "The Sexual Dynamics of Slavery."

30. Lori Ginzberg, *Women and the Work of Benevolence: Morality, Politics, and Class in the Nineteenth-Century United States* (New Haven: Yale University Press, 1990); Sylvia Hoffert, *When Hens Crow: The Women's Rights Movement in Antebellum America* (Bloomington: Indiana University Press, 1995); Rebecca Edwards, *Angels in the Machinery: Gender in American Party Politics from the Civil War to the Progressive Era* (New York: Oxford University Press, 1997); Julie Roy Jeffrey, *The Great Silent Army of Abolitionism: Ordinary Women in the Antislavery Movement* (Chapel Hill : University of North Carolina Press, 1998).

31. Madelyn Shaw and Lynn Zacek Bassett, *Homefront and Battlefield: Quilts and Content in the Civil War* (Lowell, MA: American Textile History Museum, 2012).

32. His descendants donated this pristine item (unused and intact) to the Atlanta History Center in 1990.

33. Alongside statistics and sabers, new and vibrant perspectives promote a parade of reinterpretations. See Shaw and Bassett, *Homefront and Battlefield*: we can fully appreciate Lucinda Ward Houstain's inclusion of African Americans as well as Jefferson Davis (and his daughter) into her cloth account of Civil War America at war's end.

34. Catherine Clinton, *Tara Revisited: Women, War, and the Plantation Legend* (New York: Abbeville, 1995), 142.

35. Don Siegel's 1971 film *The Beguiled* ironically illuminates the havoc taking in a wounded Yankee wreaks in a girls' boarding school in the Deep South during the Civil War. Siegel's drama does not illuminate Confederate protocol but is a Southern Gothic, replete with both playful and misogynistic themes. See Vladimir Tumanov, "One Adam and Nine Eves in Donald Siegel's *The Beguiled* and Giovanni Boccaccio's 3:1 of the Decameron," *Neophilologus* 98, no. 1 (January 2014): 1–12.

36. In Clinton and Silber, *Battle Scars*.

37. Clinton, *Tara Revisited*, 85.

38. Ibid., 85–86.

39. Ibid., 89.

40. Ibid., 84–85.

41. Kate Cumming, *Kate: The Journal of a Confederate Nurse*, ed. Richard Barksdale Harwell (1866; Baton Rouge: LSU Press, 1998), and Phoebe Yates Pember, *A Southern Woman's Story*, intro. by George Rable (Columbia: University of South Carolina Press, 2002). See also Ada Bacot, *A Confederate Nurse: The Diary of Ada W. Bacot, 1860–1863*, ed. Jean Berlin (Columbia: University of South Carolina Press, 2000).

42. Fannie Beers, *Memories: A Record of Personal Experience and Adventure During Four Years of War* (Philadelphia: J. B. Lippincott, 1891), 117.

43. Clinton, *Tara Revisited*, 89.

44. Perhaps she was paying homage to Charlotte Cushman (1816–1876), who established herself as the greatest American actress to play Shakespearean roles, touring the country successfully from 1835 until 1852, when she retired from the stage.

45. As reported in the *New York Times*, June 3, 1864.

46. Tom Tierney, *Famous African American Women: Paper Dolls* (New York: Dover, 1994). Despite the claim: "At Dover, we take paper dolls seriously. Our authors—including the world-famous Tom Tierney—thoroughly research their subjects before the sketching even starts. So each doll and outfit is accurately illustrated to the finest detail. Many of our books also feature biographies, descriptive captions, and other valuable historical information." Dover Books has not responded to my correspondence requesting information and challenging this inclusion.

47. Clinton, *Tara Revisited*, 91.

48. Ibid.

49. Ibid.

50. Rose O'Neal Greenhow, *My Imprisonment and the First Year of Abolition Rule at Washington* (London: R. Bentley, 1863), 96. See also Ann Blackman, *Wild Rose: The True Story of a Civil War Spy* (New York: Random House, 2008).

51. Clinton, *Tara Revisited*, 93–95.

52. Greenhow, *My Imprisonment*, 103.

53. H. Donald Winkler, *Stealing Secrets: How a Few Daring Women Deceived Generals, Impacted Battles, and Altered the Course of the Civil War* (Nashville, TN: Cumberland House, 2010), 258.

54. George Rable, "Missing in Action: Women and the Confederacy," in Catherine Clinton and Nina Silber, eds., *Divided Houses: Gender and the Civil War* (New York: Oxford University Press, 1995), 138.

55. New Orleans diarists suggested that "true" southern women would treat Union soldiers with disdain and not resort to the vulgar rudeness of the lower classes. Massey, *Bonnet Brigades*, 229. James Parton, *General Butler in New Orleans: History of the Administration for the Department of the Gulf in the Year 1862* (Boston: Houghton Mifflin, 1868), 327.

56. Rable, "Missing," 101.

57. Elliott Ashkenazi, ed., *The Civil War Diary of Clara Solomon: Growing Up in New Orleans, 1861–1862* (Baton Rouge: LSU Press, 1995), 419–20.

58. Rable, "Missing," 101.

59. Catherine Clinton, ed., *Mary Chesnut's Diary* (New York: Penguin, 2011), 165.

60. Parton, *General Butler*, 326.

61. Ibid., 327, 328.

62. Massey, *Bonnet Brigades*, 229–30.

63. "Journal of Mrs. Eugenia Levy Phillips, 1861–1862," www.jewish-history.com/civilwar/eugenia.html.

64. See Blackman, *Wild Rose*.

65. The 150th anniversary of her burial near Wilmington merited a ceremony. See www.whatsonwilmington.com/event.php?id=17334.

66. Margaret Johnson Erwin, *Like Some Green Laurel: Letters of Margaret Johnson Erwin, 1821–1863* (Baton Rouge, LSU Press, 1981), 127. She added with some disdain: "For that is all the gallant men are doing. Fighting for a Cause? The only causes are still Greed, Intolerance, and Insanity."

67. Belle Boyd, *Belle Boyd in Camp and Prison,* intro. by Sharon Kennedy-Nolle and foreword by Drew Gilpin Faust (1865: reprint, Baton Rouge: LSU Press, 1998), xi.

68. www.civilwar.org/education/history/biographies/maria-belle-boyd.html.

69. Sharon Kennedy-Nolle, introduction to *Belle Boyd in Camp and Prison*, 1, 3.

70. Ibid.

71. Boyd, *Belle Boyd in Camp and Prison*, 133.

72. Ibid., 46.

73. Catherine Clinton, "Wife V. Widow: Clashing Perspectives on Mary Lincoln's Legacy," *Journal of the Abraham Lincoln Association* 28, no. 1 (Winter 2007): 1.

74. Boyd, *Belle Boyd in Camp and Prison*, 84.

75. Kennedy-Nolle, introduction to *Belle Boyd in Camp and Prison*, 11.

76. On July 19, 1862, the *Philadelphia Inquirer* railed against women spies: "they are introduced under assumed names to our officers. . . . By such means they are enabled frequently to meet combinedly, but at separate times, the officers of every regiment in a whole column, and by simple compilation and comparation [*sic*] of notes, they achieve full knowledge of our entire force." Kennedy-Nolle, intro. to Boyd, *Belle Boyd*, 21–22.

77. Ibid., 17.

78. Ibid., 18.

79. Ibid., 12.

80. Ibid., 13.

81. See Drew Gilpin Faust, *Mothers of Invention: Women of the Slaveholding South in the American Civil War* (Chapel Hill: University of North Carolina Press, 1996).

82. Mary Livermore, *My Story of the War* (Hartford, CT: A. D. Worthington, 1896), 120.

83. From DeAnne Blanton, "Women Soldiers of the Civil War, Part 3," *Prologue Magazine* 25, no. 1 (Spring 1993). See documents numbered 158003, Records and Pension Office file 184934, RG 94, National Archives, Washington, DC.

84. Blanton, "Women Soldiers of the Civil War, Part 3." Wiley and Massey quoted in Blanton.

85. D. C. Bloomer, ed., *Life and Writings of Amelia Bloomer* (Boston: Arena, 1895), 336.

86. Gerrit Smith to Elizabeth C. Stanton, December 1, 1855, in *History of Woman Suffrage*, ed. Elizabeth Cady Stanton, Susan B. Anthony, and Matilda Joslyn Gage (New York: Fowler and Wells, 1881), appendix to chapter 13, 836–39, cited in Nancy Isenberg, *Sex and Citizenship in Antebellum America* (Chapel Hill: University of North Carolina Press, 1998), 54.

87. Catherine Clinton, *Fanny Kemble's Civil Wars* (New York: Simon and Schuster, 2000).

88. www.washingtonpost.com/wp-dyn/content/article/2007/12/08/AR2007120801502 .html.

89. Blanton and Cook, *They Fought Like Demons*, 25–26.

90. Catherine Clinton "Public Women and Sexual Politics During the American Civil War," in Clinton and Silber, *Battle Scars*.

### CHAPTER THREE

1. Audre Lorde, "The Master's Tools Will Never Dismantle the Master's House" (1984), in Lorde, *Sister Outsider: Essays and Speeches* (Berkeley, CA: Crossing Press, 2007), 110–14.

2. The title of Lorde's work is *Zami: A New Spelling of My Name A Biomythography* (Berkeley, CA: Crossing Point Press, 1982). See bell hooks, *Talking Back: Thinking Feminist,*

Notes to Pages 76–83

*Thinking Black* (Boston: South End Press, 1989), 15. Ironically, it may be "bio-mythography" that white southern women at the turn of the twentieth century were practicing without any consciousness of it, as they were struggling with issues of reunion and release.

3. Hooks, *Talking Back*, 166.

4. Phil Patton, "Mammy: Her Life and Times," www.ferris.edu/jimcrow/links/mammy/homepage.htm.

5. The campaign to put a woman on American paper money has a long genesis, but the recent campaign stemmed from a grassroots movements called "Women on the Twenties" (which conducted Internet polls, with results from over 600,000 participants voting in March 2015), in combination with an effort within the U.S. Treasury, "The New Ten," which generated over a million responses on the Treasury website. Secretary of Treasury Jacob Lew has promised a new "family of bills" in April 2016, with multiple women on the back of new designs for the five dollar and ten dollar bill, and one woman—Tubman—on the front of the $20.

6. The campaign to put a woman on the currency was complicated and delayed by debates over which historical figure might be removed in any redesign; these centered on a contest between Alexander Hamilton and Andrew Jackson.

7. See Cheryl Sattler, *Teaching to Transcend: Educating Women Against Violence* (Albany: State University of New York, 2000), and see clinics and shelters in Minneapolis, Chicago, and Washington. For a fictional treatment of the "new" underground railroad, see Anna Quindlen, *Black and Blue* (New York: Random House, 1998). This phenomenon parallels and has a direct linkage with groups and movements such as "Mothers Against Raping Children," which created clandestine safe houses and sanctuaries as well. "Secret Network Helps Children Flee Sex Abuse," www.nytimes.com/1988/06/20/us/secret-network-helps-children-flee-sex-abuse.html.

8. Earl Conrad, *Harriet Tubman* (Washington, DC: Associated Press, 1943), 172–73.

9. Ibid.

10. *Boston Commonwealth*, July 17, 1863.

11. Besides the aforementioned work by Jean Fagan Yellin on Harriet Jacobs, see also Elsa Barkley Brown, "Constructing a Life and a Community: A Partial Story of Maggie Lena Walker," *OAH Magazine of History* 7, no. 4 (1993): 28–31, and Mia Bay's introduction to Ida B. Wells-Barnett, *The Light of Truth: Writings of an Anti-Lynching Crusader* (New York: Penguin, 2014). Both Walker and Wells-Barnett were born during the Civil War. There is more work on northern black women during this period; see Brenda Stevenson on Charlotte Forten or Margaret Washington and Nell Irvin Painter on Sojourner Truth.

12. Susie King Taylor, *Reminiscences of My Life in Camp with the 33d United States Colored Troops, Late 1st S. C. Volunteers* (Boston, 1902), and Catherine Clinton, ed., *Reminiscences of My Life in Camp: An African American Woman's Civil War Memoir,* by Susie King Taylor (Athens: University of Georgia Press, 2006).

126

13. No black women were included in Ken Burns's "The Civil War" final episode, in his summation program tracing lives after the war—only a handful of African Americans and women combined made this select circle.

14. Clinton, *Reminiscences of My Life*, 32.

15. Ibid.

16. Ibid., 104.

17. See Catherine Clinton, *The Plantation Mistress: Woman's World in the Old South* (New York: Pantheon, 1982).

18. Micki McElya, *Clinging to Mammy: The Faithful Slave in Twentieth-Century America* (Cambridge, MA: Harvard University Press, 2007), 5.

19. See Catherine Clinton, *Tara Revisited: Women, War, and the Plantation Legend* (New York: Abbeville, 1995), 23.

20. Harriet Beecher Stowe, *Uncle Tom's Cabin* (Boston: John Jewett and Co., 1852), 20.

21. Sheri Parks, *Fierce Angels: The Strong Black Woman in American Life and Culture* (New York: Ballantine, 2010), 46.

22. Trudier Harris, *From Mammies to Militants: Domestics in Black American Literature* (Philadelphia, PA: Temple University Press, 1982). See also Diane Roberts, *The Myth of Aunt Jemima: Representations of Race and Region* (New York: Routledge, 1994), and Ronald L. Jackson II, *Scripting the Black Masculine Body: Identity, Discourse, and Racial Politics in Popular Media* (Albany, SUNY Press, 2006), 38.

23. "The mammy is another figure in the pantheon that is confounded by a scripted identity matrix." Jackson, *Scripting*, 38.

24. K. Sue Jewell, *From Mammy To Miss America and Beyond: Cultural Images and the Shaping of U.S. Social Policy* (New York, Routledge, 1993), 37. See also Roberts, *Myth*, and Patricia Turner, *Ceramic Uncles and Celluloid Mammies: Black Images and Their Influence on Culture* (New York: Anchor Books, 1994).

25. Cynthia Mills and Pamela H. Simpson, eds., *Monuments to the Lost Cause: Women, Art, and the Landscapes of Southern Memory* (Knoxville: University of Tennessee Press, 2003).

26. See, e.g., "We are introduced to Josephine, the baby niece of President Woodrow Wilson, who is allegedly 'in possession of a real colored mammy.'" McElya, *Clinging to Mammy*, 126. See also Tony Horwitz, "The Mammy Washington Almost Had," www.theatlantic.com/national/archive/2013/05/the-mammy-washington-almost-had/276431.

27. Kimberly Wallace-Sanders, *Mammy: A Century of Race, Gender, and Southern Memory* (Ann Arbor: University of Michigan Press, 2008), 3.

28. The term *maverick* comes from a nineteenth-century Texan rancher, Samuel A. Maverick, who failed to brand his cattle; thus his calves became known as "mavericks."

29. The third and middle ground, Scottish Gaelic, has many and multiple outlets. But it should not be confused with the Scots language, which is of Germanic origin and is sometimes called Lowland Scots or Ulster Scots. This language is studied, preserved, and

spoken in Scotland and Northern Ireland. Scotland has 790 offshore islands, which presents quite a linguistic laboratory for specialists but a real earful for scholars.

30. Irish linguists are fond of deriding "telly terms," which are words derived from modern media, like television, rather than spoken lore. But in some ways, I wonder if television and/or YouTube keeps spoken language alive in the wake of a creeping monotony of sameness. Certainly, accents and dialects are much more prevalent within the broadcast world than they are in cyberspace. It would be a decidedly fantastic mash-up to bring the Celtic to the Cajun, as was done when the American Conference for Irish Studies met in New Orleans on St. Patrick's Day in 2012.

31. See www.officialkwanzaawebsite.org/index.shtml (the founder's official website) and Elizabeth Pleck, "Kwanzaa: The Making of a Black Nationalist Tradition, 1966–1990," *Journal of American Ethnic History* 20, no. 4 (Summer 2001): 3–28.

32. *Jumping the Broom* is a magazine and a film title. On websites such as African American Roots, Inc., you can purchase "heritage wedding brooms" and accessories, or you can order a custom-made broom on Etsy.

33. See www.urbandictionary.com/define.php?term=mammy.

34. Al Jolson's multilayered performance within this drama played on the theme of hidden identities, of "masking." In the original version of the film, the jazz singer wears blackface. The film's plot involves a rebellious cantor's son who rejects his Jewish roots and directs his talent toward a secular singing career, against his father's wishes. The storyline includes a melodramatic scene of reconciliation when the son sings the "Kol Nidre" while his father is ailing and earns paternal approval before his father's death. The final scene shows his mother happily reconciled while watching him perform "Mammy" on Broadway. Ironically, Al Jolson was one of the first American entertainers to gain prominence on stage and screen who openly embraced his own Jewish identity, while he blacked up his face in an era when African American actors were rarely allowed on-screen.

35. Richard Corliss, *Time*, Oct. 24, 2011. "Mammy" had been introduced on the vaudeville stage by William Frawley, who later played *I Love Lucy*'s Fred Mertz.

36. Randall Kennedy, *Nigger: The Strange Career of a Troublesome Word* (New York: Pantheon, 2001).

37. Mammy's descendant "Aunt Jemima" is rarely invoked; it does not have anywhere near the same punch.

38. See www.petitiononline.com/aj461153/petition.html.

39. Still, it was such a shock, if not an obscenity, for me to find myself surrounded by "Mammy" banners, cakes, and candies in twenty-first-century Ireland.

40. A direct contrast to women such as Ellen Glasgow, among others.

41. Jewell, *From Mammy to Miss America,* 37.

42. Parks, *Fierce Angels,* 40.

43. Roberts, *Myth.*

44. McElya, *Clinging to Mammy,* and Wallace-Sanders, *Mammy.*

45. Horwitz, "The Mammy."

46. Eugene Genovese, *Roll, Jordan, Roll: The World the Slaves Made* (New York: Pantheon, 1975), 417.

47. Clinton, *Plantation Mistress*, 212–13.

48. Catherine Clinton, "Breaking the Silence: Sexual Hypocrisies from Thomas Jefferson to Strom Thurmond," in Bernadette Brooten, ed., *Beyond Slavery: Overcoming Its Religious and Sexual Legacies* (New York: Palgrave, 2010).

49. I still think the idea of predators is something to which I might return, but perhaps leaving Thomas Jefferson out of it.

50. I look forward especially to a new anthology edited by Daina Ramey Berry and Leslie Harris, *Sexuality and Slavery: Creating an Intimate History of the Americas* (Athens: University of Georgia Press, forthcoming).

51. Thavolia Glymph, *Out of the House of Bondage: The Transformation of the Plantation Household* (New York: Cambridge University Press, 2008). Glymph's work, of course, built on earlier studies as well, including Leslie Schwalm's *A Hard Fight for We: Women's Transition from Slavery to Freedom in South Carolina* (Champaign-Urbana: University of Illinois Press, 1997) and Noralee Frankel's *Freedom's Women: Black Women and Families in Civil War Era Mississippi* (Bloomington: Indiana University Press, 1999).

52. Indeed, because many seemed to fundamentally misread some of my principle arguments in *The Plantation Mistress: Women's World in the Old South* (1982), I prepared a focused essay on women's relations in the slaveholder's household entitled "Caught in the Web of the Big House," for Walter Fraser, ed., *The Web of Southern Social Relations: Women, Family, and Education* (Athens: University of Georgia Press, 1985). The essay has been anthologized in both Paul Finkelman's *Articles on American Slavery* (1990) and Darlene Clark Hine's *Black Women in History* (2005). In this essay, to dispel the notion of perpetually harmonious slaveholding households, I offer compelling examples, including a jealous plantation mistress who cuts off the head of a baby fathered by her husband with his enslaved concubine.

53. Throughout her book, Glymph subtly undermines the claim that Drew Gilpin Faust made in her authoritative study, *Mothers of Invention* (1996). Glymph suggests that the problematic function of Faust's thesis (part of an argument that Marli F. Weiner made in *Mistresses and Slaves: Plantation Women in South Carolina, 1830–80* [Urbana-Champaign: University of Illinois, 1998]) and subsequent studies of planter women is the assumption that the Civil War was, in fact, a defining moment in which slaveholding women emerged as principal actors in nineteenth-century southern history.

54. I would suggest there was a subset of white women who felt rightly displaced within their own households and resented the way in which their husbands might subvert lines of authority. See, e.g., Catherine Hammond, wife of James Henry Hammond, who absented herself from her husband's household not when he took up illicit sexual relations with an enslaved woman but when he took as a concubine the twelve-year-old daughter

of his former concubine. See Clinton, "Caught in the Web of the Big House." Letters and especially divorce petitions in the antebellum era were filled with complaints that men allowed liaisons with African American women to displace white female authority—which in some cases produced white female violence.

55. Ta-Nehisi Coates, *Between the World and Me* (New York: Spiegel and Grau, 2015).

56. www.freedmen.umd.edu/rice.htm.

57. Clinton, *Tara Revisited*, 74.

58. Peter Bardaglio, "The Children of Jubilee," in Catherine Clinton and Nina Silber, eds., *Divided Houses: Gender and the Civil War* (New York: Oxford University Press, 1995), 221.

59. See Catherine Clinton, "'With a Whip in his Hand:' Rape, Memory and African-American Women," in Geneviève Fabre and Robert O'Meally, eds., *History and Memory in African-American Culture* (New York: Oxford University Press, 1994), and Catherine Clinton, "Reconstructing Freedwomen," in Clinton and Silber, *Divided Houses*.

60. Catherine Clinton, *The Other Civil War: American Women in the Nineteenth Century* (1984; rev. ed., New York: Hill and Wang, 1999), 171.

61. Ibid.

62. Elna C. Green, ed., *Lily Hardy Hammond in Black and White: An Interpretation of the South* (Athens: University of Georgia Press, 2010).

63. Lily H. Hammond, *Southern White Women and Racial Adjustment* (Lynchburg, VA: J. P. Bell Co., 1917). See also Angelina Grimke, *An Appeal to the Christian Women of the South* (New York: American Antislavery Society, 1836), available at http://utc.iath.virginia.edu/abolitn/abesaegat.html.

64. Diane Miller Sommerville, *Rape and Race in the Nineteenth-Century South* (Chapel Hill: University of North Carolina Press, 2004).

65. Annette Gordon Reed, "Histories Distorted," in Roundtable, "One Family's History: A Nation's History," *New York Times*, October 8, 2009, http://roomfordebate.blogs.nytimes.com/2009/10/08/one-familys-roots-a-nations-history.

66. Fabre and O'Meally, *History and Memory*.

67. Ida B. Wells-Barnett, "The Reason Why the Colored American is Not at the Columbian Exposition," http://digital.library.upenn.edu/women/wells/exposition/exposition.html. See Mia Bay, *To Tell the Truth Freely: The Life of Ida Wells-Barnett* (New York: Hill and Wang, 2010), and Sarah Silkey, *Black Woman Reformer: Ida B. Wells, Lynching, and Transatlantic Activism* (Athens: University of Georgia Press, 2015).

68. Kenneth Goings, *Mammy and Uncle Mose: Black Collectibles and American Stereotyping* (Bloomington: Indiana University Press, 1994), 31. See also Turner, *Ceramic Uncles*. We have no evidence that the general went back to share some of the profits with this wonderful cook, as the company sold for over $4 million in the 1920s.

69. Maurice Manring, *Slave in a Box: The Strange Career of Aunt Jemima* (Charlottesville: University of Virginia, 1998).

70. Jewell, *From Mammy to Miss America*, 37.

71. See http://journalofthecivilwarera.org/forum-the-future-of-civil-war-era-studies/the-future-of-civil-war-era-studies-race.

72. With apologies to Walter Fleming, after whom these lectures were named, and with gratitude to Jim Downs whose generosity during the preparation of these lectures was invaluable.

73. Mike Konczal, "How Radical Change Occurs: An Interview with Eric Foner," *Nation*, February 3, 2015.

74. Mary P. Ryan, *Mysteries of Sex: Tracing Women and Men Through American History* (Chapel Hill: University of North Carolina Press, 2006), 129.

75. Frankel, *Freedom's Women*, 25.

76. Mary Farmer-Kaiser, *Freedwomen and the Freedmen's Bureau: Race, Gender, and Public Policy in the Age of Emancipation* (New York, Fordham University Press, 2010), 64.

77. See Barbara Christian, *Black Women Novelists: The Development of a Tradition, 1892–1976* (Westport, CT: Greenwood, 1980).

78. In June 2015, a woman sparked a national controversy when she was "outed" masquerading as a woman of color, teaching as a black woman in Africana Studies at Eastern Washington University, and serving as president of the Spokane chapter of the NAACP. Forced to resign her position and defend her identity politics, critics claimed she was a white woman "in blackface," while others who have suggested that race is a "construction," not a fixed definition, were drawn into debates. See Rachel Dolezal case.

79. Carol Manning, *The Female Tradition in Southern Literature* (Urbana-Champaign: University of Illinois Press, 1993), 31.

80. See Mel Watkins, "Sexism, Racism and Black Women Writers," *New York Times*, June 15, 1986.

81. Saidiya Hartman, *Lose Your Mother: A Journey Along the Atlantic Slave Route* (New York: Farrar, Straus, Giroux, 2008). I would suggest that Diane McWhorter's *Carry Me Home: Birmingham, Alabama, The Climactic Battle of the Civil Rights Revolution* (New York: Simon and Schuster, 2001) is another example of "breaking the wall" to blend memoir and history effectively.

82. http://legalhistoryblog.blogspot.com/2012/01/blogging-aha-kornbluh-on-welke-telling.html.

83. See, e.g., Jennifer Morgan, *Laboring Women: Gender and Reproduction in New World Slavery* (Philadelphia: University of Pennsylvania Press, 2004), and Tera Hunter, *To 'Joy My Freedom': Southern Black Women's Lives and Labors After the Civil War* (Cambridge, MA: Harvard University Press, 1997).

84. With a shout-out to my former student and dynamic scholar, Zaheer Ali.

85. On the Freedom volumes, see www.freedmen.umd.edu/fsppubs.htm. Deborah Gray White, *Aren't I a Woman: Female Slaves in the Plantation South* (New York: Norton, 1985); Jacqueline Jones, *Labor of Love, Labor of Sorrow: Black Women, Work, and the Family*

from *Slavery to the Present* (New York: Basic, 1985); Schwalm, *A Hard Fight for We*; and Jean Fagan Yellin, *Harriet Jacobs: A Life* (New York: Basic, 2005).

86. Clinton, *Tara Revisited,* 72.

87. Jean Fagan Yellin, ed., *Incidents in the Life of a Slave Girl Written by Herself* (Cambridge: Harvard University Press, 1985).

88. Pauli Murray, *Proud Shoes* (New York: Harpers, 1956).

89. First published by Lee and Shepard in Boston in 1868, reprinted by the Arno Press in 1969.

90. Carla Peterson, *Black Gotham: A Family History of African Americans in Nineteenth Century New York City* (New Haven, CT: Yale University Press, 2011).

91. Hubert H. McAlexander, *The Prodigal Daughter: A Biography of Sherwood Bonner* (Baton Rouge: LSU Press, 1981).

92. For the best new account of this movement, consult Isabel Wilkerson's *The Warmth of Other Suns: The Epic Story of America's Great Migration* (New York: Random House, 2010).

93. "In First Lady's Roots, A Complex Path from Slavery," *New York Times,* October 7, 2009, www.nytimes.com/2009/10/08/us/politics/08genealogy.html. See also Rachel Swarns, *American Tapestry: The Story of the Black, White, and Multiracial Ancestors of Michelle Obama* (New York: Amistad, 2012).

94. The story of Michelle Obama's forebears, particularly Melvina, was lost to her until the genealogical research of Megan Smolenyak was able to trace these ancestors and provide Obama with evidence of nineteenth-century family lore.

95. Parks, *Fierce Angels,* 40.

96. This issue was covered by the *New York Times,* the *Atlantic,* and dozens of historical and social media blogs. See, e.g., "The Mommy/Mammy Issues in *The Help.* https://acritical reviewofthehelp.wordpress.com/2011/03/02/mommy-mammy-issue. Ida E. Jones, the national director of the Association of Black Women Historians, released an open statement criticizing the film, stating, "*The Help* distorts, ignores, and trivializes the experiences of black domestic workers." www.abwh.org/images/pdf/TheHelp-Statement.pdf.

97. Schwalm, *A Hard Fight for We,* 147.

98. For other examples, please see Catherine Clinton, "Reconstructing Freedwomen," in Clinton and Silber, *Divided Houses.*

99. Horwitz, "The Mammy."

100. Mammy is always depicted as old and overweight, contrary to all evidence that childminders were often young girls in the plantation household. See Clinton, *The Plantation Mistress,* 201–3.

101. Elna C. Green, ed., *Lily Hardy Hammond in Black and White: An Interpretation of the South* (Athens: University of Georgia Press, 2010), xxxvii.

102. Davis made this statement in her October 2015 acceptance speech for winning an Emmy. She is developing a project on Harriet Tubman and intends to play the lead in an

HBO film. http://variety.com/2015/tv/news/viola-davis-harriet-tubman-hbo-kirk-ellis-movie-1201480848.

103. David Pilgrim, Ferris State University, 2008, edited 2012, www.ferris.edu/HTMLS/news/jimcrow/sapphire.

104. http://creativetime.org/projects/karawalker/curatorial-statement.

105. See Hilton Als, "The Sugar Sphinx," *New Yorker,* May 8, 2014, www.newyorker.com/culture/culture-desk/the-sugar-sphinx.

106. Gloria Malone, "What Kara Walker's Sugar Baby Showed Us," http://rhrealitycheck.org/article/2014/07/21/kara-walkers-sugar-baby-showed-us.

107. Scholars and activists are challenging the media to incorporate women's names into their reporting and analysis. The "Black Lives Matter" movement was shaped by women activists who want their concerns reflected. See www.dissentmagazine.org/article/women-black-lives-matter-interview-marcia-chatelain and also www.npr.org/2015/10/12/447911196/critics-say-women-are-neglected-by-black-lives-matter-campaign.

108. www.aapf.org/sayhernamereport.

# INDEX

"African American Women in the Literary Imagination of Mary Boykin Chesnut" (Glymph), 28

African Americans: exceptionalism of African American women, 82; as hospital attendants during the Civil War, 56; portrayal of as robust political actors during the Civil War, 101–3; revisionist historical work concerning, 93; as Union soldiers, 79. *See also* women, African American, southern; slavery/slaves

Ainsworth, F. C., 71

antebellum estates, 95

Antigone, 3

Appomattox, Confederate surrender at, 22

archival research, 104–6; and the possibilities of social change, 102

*At the Mercy of Tiberius* (Evans), 11

Aunt Jemima, 90, 100–101

"Aunt Rosy's Chest" (Wadsworth), 107

Avery, Myrta Lockett, 32

Banks, Nathaniel, 73

*Battle Cry of Freedom* (McPherson), 8

"Battle of the Handkerchiefs," 74

*Battle Scars: Gender and Sexuality in the American Civil War* (ed. C. Clinton and Silber), 106

Beauregard, P. G. T., 35, 60

Beavers, Louise, 101

Beers, Fannie, 57

*Beguiled* (1971), 123n35

Belle Boyd. *See* Boyd, Maria Isabella

*Belle Boyd in Camp and Prison* (Boyd), 68–69

Berry, Daina Ramey, 99

*Between the World and Me* (Coates), 95

*Beulah* (Evans), 9

bio-mythography, 85, 125–26n2

*Birth of a Nation* (1915), 108–9

*Black Gotham: A Family History of African Americans in Nineteenth Century New York City* (Peterson), 106

Black Lives Matter movement, 133n107

Blanton, DeAnne, 42, 71

Blight, David, 98

*Blood and Irony: Southern White Women's Narratives of the Civil War, 1861–1937* (Gardner), 9

Bloomer, Amelia, 72

Bonham, Milledge, 60

Boyd, Maria Isabella (Belle Boyd), 66–70; dual nature (hybridity) of her espionage/military activities, 67–68; gender issues concerning, 68, 69–70; marriages of, 68, 69; as a professional actress and Lost Cause champion, 68–69

Bradford, Sarah, 78